A HISTORY OF THORNHILL

Hugh Allaynson, 1379 p.7

1. The "Cross", at the junction of Combs Road, Overthrope Road and The Town, April 1995. A wooden cross is erected on this site at Easter each year, but this is the site of the Market Cross and is the oldest part of the village of Thornhill, see plan of Medieval Thornhill on page 24. (GJ)

A HISTORY OF THORNHILL
by **Barbara H. Nuttall**

and

A Guide to the Church of St. Michael And All Angels

by Barbara Nutall updated
by Revd Ronald W. F. Howell

Published jointly by:

Kirklees Cultural Services and Thornhill Church Council

Kirklees Cultural Services
Red Doles Lane
Huddersfield
HD2 1YF

1st Edition 1970
2nd Edition 1987
3rd Edition 1995

© 1995

ISBN 0 900746 61 0

Kirklees Cultural Services are not responsible for the materials and opinions contained herein, which are the responsibility of the author.

All rights reserved. No part of this publication may be reproduced in any form, by any means, electronic, mechanical photocopying, recording or otherwise, without the prior permission of the publishers.

Printed by Titus Wilson, Kendal in Plantin typeface on High-speed Blade, 100gm^2.

CONTENTS

A HISTORY OF THORNHILL

page

Foreword	vii
From the Beginning	1
Early Civilization and Settlement	2
The Domesday Survey and the Thornhill Manor	4
Medieval Thornhill	5
The Later Middle Ages	7
The Savile Family	10
The Villages and Village Life	20
The Parish Registers	26
The Vestry Accounts	29
A Century of Change	33
The Nineteenth Century	37
Conclusion	43

A GUIDE TO THE CHURCH OF ST. MICHAEL AND ALL ANGELS

Thornhill Church	48
The Nave	49
The Chancel	50
The Savile Chapel	51
The South Chapel	54
Choir Vestry	54
South Aisle	54
The Tower	55
Porch	56
Parish Chest	56
Outside	57
Glossary	58
Bibliography	60
Index	61

ILLUSTRATIONS

A HISTORY OF THORNHILL

1. Thornhill "Cross" — ii
2. Anglo Saxon stone monuments — 3
3. Jordan, son of Essolf — 6
4. The Savile Chapel — 11
5. Thornhill Hall and surroundings, c.1600 — 12
6. Lady Anne Savile, 1634 — 14
7. Thornhill in 1634 — 16
8. View across the moat c.1910 — 21
9. Remains of Thornhill Hall. — 22
10. Medieval Thornhill — 24
11. Savile Arms and Church Lane — 39
12. Thornhill Pageant, 1952 — 44

GUIDE TO THE CHURCH OF ST. MICHAEL AND ALL ANGELS

13. The Nave
14. Thornhill Church
15. Plan of Thornhill Church
16. Sir John Savile Monument
17. Thornhill Church Communion Plate

ILLUSTRATION AND PHOTOGRAPH CREDITS

Photographs and illustrations are copyright and reproduced by permission of the following:

- (Ex) Huddersfield Daily Examiner
- (GJ) George Jackson LRPS
- (KCS) Kirklees Cultural Services
- (KMC) Kirklees Metropolitan Council
- (LS) Lord Savile
- (NAS) Nottinghamshire Archive Service
- (S) Singleton Collection, Kirklees Cultural Ser
- (SC) Smith Carter Collection, Kirklees Cultural Services
- (V & A) Victoria and Albert Museum
- (WYAS) West Yorkshire Archaeological Service.

FOREWORD

Barbara Nuttall's first edition of the combined *History of Thornhill and the Guide to the Church* was published by Thornhill Parish Church Council in 1970. Unavailable for a number of years it was republished as a joint effort by Kirklees Libraries, Museums and Arts and Thornhill Church Council.

The history in the 1987 edition was basically a photographic copy of the 1970 version with the addition of some new text and an extended Conclusion. The Guide was similarly updated to include recent church acquisitions and alterations. The Guide was based largely on one first published in 1940 written by Tom Charlesworth. Mr Charlesworth was the headmaster of the C of E Boys' School from 1893 to 1923. His life-long interest in Thornhill Church and his willingness to share his knowledge about it was an important influence on Mrs Nuttall's own early enthusiasm for local history.

In 1978 part of Thornhill in the vicinity of the church and the old Hall was designated by Kirklees Council as a special area for conservation. This underlines its value to the district from the point of view of his history and of how people built here in the past. The buildings involved are a closely connected group - church, parsonage, inn, Hall, farm and smaller houses - and now, with care from local people and the Council it should be possible to enjoy their special atmosphere for many years to come.

Mrs Nuttall died in 1990 and since the booklet was out of print it was decided to reprint the main text and update the *Guide to Thornhill Church* including some of the changes that have taken place in recent years. Kirklees Cultural Services are grateful to Revd Ron Howell for his assistance in rewriting the *Guide* to the church; to Yorkshire Archaeological Society and Nottinghamshire Archive Service for their help in tracing illustrations that were previously used in the book; Lord Savile for his kindness in allowing Mrs Nuttall to use his family papers and us to rephotograph the portrait of Lady Anne Savile and the 1634 map of the Thornhill Estate; Liz Hayes and George Jackson for the new photographs. A special mention must be made of Dr H G Wayment who allowed us to use his, as yet unpublished, research on the Savile Chapel and Sir John Savile to add a few extra facts to Mrs Nuttall's text.

We have taken this opportunity of resetting the text to bring the various alterations closer together, and to include some extra photographs. We trust that Mrs Nuttall (and her family) would appreciate the changes made and are sure that she would have been pleased to see the book in print once again.

Isobel Schofield (editor)

A HISTORY OF THORNHILL
by Barbara H. Nuttall

From the beginning

The village of Thornhill, near Dewsbury, in West Riding of Yorkshire, lies on a projecting ridge of the eastern edge of the Pennines. The top of the ridge is a plateau which is roughly triangular in shape. To the north and east its hillsides rise from the valley of the Calder; to the south, from the valley of Howroyd Beck and Smithy and Brook.

The word village used of modern Thornhill is, strictly speaking, a misnomer, for since 1910 it has been part of the county borough of Dewsbury. Consequently it has increasingly acquired suburban characteristics, but it has a long, independent and interesting history of its own. Even today because of its position – about 200 to 300 feet higher above sea level than Dewsbury, two miles away and separated from it by the river and a number of surviving fields – it still keeps it own clear identity.

Approximately 20,000 years ago, and for a vast amount of time before that, England north of the Thames was largely covered by ice but geologists believe that a large lake, which did not freeze, filled most of the Calder valley. It extended, of course, some way up the Calder's tributaries so that, whilst the site on which the centre of Dewsbury now stands would necessarily be below the water, the highest part of Thornhill's ridge would be a thin tongue of land jutting into the lake.

During the Old Stone Age the weather became warmer and the snows melted. Probably the Pennines provided food and occasional shelter to some of the nomadic tribes living in the area. These people lived by hunting on the high ground, and some of their flint tools have been found in a few places in Yorkshire. But it is not until the Mesolithic or Middle Stone Age, that flint tools are found in this part of the Pennines in any quantity.

The Middle Stone Age lasted, roughly, from 12,000 BC to 2,300 BC is noted for tiny flint implements called Microliths, which the people of those times – apparently fowlers and fishers as well as hunters – left behind them. These pygmy flints have been found extensively in Yorkshire, and in 1954 one which appears to be of that period was unearthed on "the Tops" of Thornhill Edge. One flint is proof of very little, but the district appears so suitable for Middle Stone Age man, that it would be surprising if digging in the right places did not turn up others. A quantity of them – giving the impression that the site was a local "workshop" – were found on Woolley Edge, only five miles from Thornhill.

Thornhill's prominent edge is a massive Middle Coal Measure sandstone, 65 feet thick, known in the area as "Thornhill Rock". Sandstones like this appear to be more congenial to medolithic people than the millstone grits of the higher central Pennines. The scenery they support is softer than that of the millstone grits; fish and fowl would be more plentiful. Naturally, early men would prefer southern aspects on the hills, and water were accessible without too much trouble then conditions were eminently suitable for a camping place. These conditions are fulfiled on the southern side of the Thornhill ridge (the "Tops" previously mentioned) where springs leave the hillside.

Therefore it is possible to date some kind of habitation of this area, even if only occasional, from mesolithic times.

The Mesolithic period was followed by the Neolithic, or New Stone Age, and then by the Bronze Age. People began to grow crops to support themselves, as well as to hunt. They developed the use of metals and Civilisation as we think of it, started. No remains of these later periods have yet been found in Thornhill, but, going forward to the Britain of Roman times, at last there is solid evidence of a settlement here.

Early civilisation and settlement

When Julius Caesar came to Britain in 55 BC the tribes he found were considerably more civilised than Stone or Bronze Age people. They grew crops, could work in iron as well as bronze, made pottery and ornaments, and carried on trade with the continent. Caesar's raids did not extend further north than the Thames, but in AD 43 a large part of the country was overrun by the Romans under the Emperor Claudius, and Roman rule was gradually extended to cover all of what is now England and Wales, and part-way into Scotland. It took until about AD 70 however, before the north of England was subdued.

At that time the mid and north Pennines were occupied by the tribe of the Brigantes. It is likely that there would be a British settlement of sorts, if only a look-out position, on the higher part of the Thornhill ridge. Its commanding situation at the entrance to the narrowing Calder valley, with extensive views both up and down the river, make this almost a certainty. At all events it is clear that someone was there a century later, for in 1939, when houses were being built in Overthorpe Avenue, a hoard of 27 silver coins, dated between AD 69 and AD 180 was found in the ground under a large stone[1]. Hoards like this turn up in many parts of the North, and they are usually connected by their dates with periods of unrest and rebellion against Roman rule. Presumably the hoard was hidden in the ground when pillage and slaughter threatened, or when the owner left his home to attack the conquerors – but was never reclaimed.

The next evidence we have of what happened in Thornhill is of a very different nature from the second century coins. It comes from a large collection of broken stones on display in the church. Found in the nineteenth century during some rebuilding of the church, these are remains of stone crosses and a stone coffin dating from the Anglo-Saxon period of our history. A number of churches in West Riding have similar fragments – in particular, Dewsbury has parts of a very fine cross indeed – but these are particularly notable for having four inscriptions amongst the pieces.

The inscriptions on the crosses are in Runes – a lettering of straight lines which it is impossible to decipher without special knowledge, but they have been translated, and show that the monuments were personal ones put up to the dead by friends or relatives. A composite model of the finest one – to a woman, Bersuith, from another woman, Gilsuith – was constructed by the Tolson Museum, Huddersfield and was on display in the church in 1995.

The fragment of the stone coffin has its inscription in Roman lettering. It dates from about AD 870 and was made for a man named Osbert. Stone coffins dating from Anglian times for an important person. For this reason it has been suggested that the coffin might have held the body of King Osbert, killed by the Danes near York in AD 867.

When the Danes invaded northern England the western parts of Yorkshire were not settled by them immediately; in fact, the Archbishop of York escaped in 867 to Wharfedale (returning to York when the Danes recognised Christianity) so that it is not impossible that the King's body also should have been brought to the west.

In any case these stones make it quite clear that there was a religious establishment of some importance at Thornhill in Anglian times. It appears to have been contemporaneous with another, perhaps even more

(1) The coins are now in the collection of Kirklees Museums and may be seen on request.

important, at Dewsbury. To this day the parishes of Thornhill, Almondbury, Kirkheaton, Bradford, and Huddersfield, pay a small amount of money yearly to the church at Dewsbury. This has been widely held to show that the parish of Dewsbury once included the whole of these districts. Further investigation of the medieval circumstances under which these payments were made seems to indicate, however, that they originated only from parts of these parishes – part which were land that had once been included in the King's Demesne.²

Up to the time of the Domesday Survey, and for a short time afterwards, Dewsbury was a Royal manor.³ Its church would receive "church scot" from royal land in the district. This was one of the oldest church taxes and was often later confused with tithes. Very likely the church at Dewsbury was a "minster", which meant, in those days, that it would send out preachers to many of the surrounding districts; but this does not mean quite the same thing as that the whole of these districts were once part of the Dewsbury parish. From the evidence of the stone fragments, the religious establishment at Thornhill seems to have been of the same period as the Dewsbury one, even if it was not as important. Was it a rival house? Or more likely, a church established by the local lord chiefly for his own people? In any case, bearing in mind the early settlement of Thornhill, might it even have been placed on ground held sacred by the native British before the time of the invasions of the Angles.

Early parishes, as the ecclesiastical units we understand, were formed mostly in the ninth and tenth centuries. At the Domesday survey in 1086 Thornhill and Dewsbury both had a church and a priest. In the fourteenth century (from accounts which survive) the tax that Thornhill paid to Dewsbury parish was then paid in the form of half the tithes of Shitlington and Flockton, two outlying parts of Thornhill parish. These two districts included plans that had once been royal demesne. It seems highly likely then, that the money now paid is a composition fee for early medieval "church scot" from them only, and that Thornhill parish is as old as Dewsbury. The same holds for some of the other places which still pay dues.

2. Anglo-Saxon stone monument of the ninth and tenth centuries. (GJ)

(2) The King's Demesne was all the land that the King kept for his own use or profit. The rest of the country was held by some of the more important or powerful of the King's subjects – chiefly, in return, for fighting for him when necessary.

(3) The word Manor (now sometimes used loosely instead of Manor House) meant the land and its appurtenances, tenants etc. held by a man, its lord, at a given place. The Lord's jurisdiction held sway in his manors, of which he might hold one or more.

The Domesday Survey and the Thornhill Manor

The Domesday Survey was undertaken for William the Conqueror in 1086. The Norman commissioners enquired about every district in the country from a number of senior members of the community and, where possible, how it compares with conditions before 1066. Their chief concern appears to have been to find out what could be taxed and, as land was the main source of wealth in those days, the survey gives enough detail of the countryside to give us surprisingly clear pictures of it. We can also get an idea of how many people inhabited each place and their standing in the social scale.

The Thornhill entry occurs in the account of extensive lands given to the Norman, Ilbert de Laci by the Conqueror. Translated into modern English, its abbreviations expanded, it reads:

> Gerneber, Aldene and Gamel had four carucates of plans for geld (tax) and three villeins and three bordars there with two ploughs. A priest is there and a church. Wood pasturable, six quarenteens in length and six in breadth. At the time of King Edward the Confessor it was worth 40s.; now 20s.

The difference in the value was possibly the result of the harrying of the North by William early in his reign. He savagely put down opposition which threatened to be violent. He burned villages, killing many of their inhabitants, with results which were still obvious twenty years later. For purposes of comparison, Dewsbury was worth 10s. both before and after 1066. Apparently it was less affected by turmoil and resettlement.

At this point it is necessary to point out that Thornhill township (or *vill*, to which the survey refers) is not the same as Thornhill Parish. The Parish covered a much greater area and included the township of Shitlington[4], Flockton, and Whitley as well. Thornhill township extended to the Calder on the north and east, and to Smithy Brook on the south. In this account I shall speak sometimes of the township and sometimes of the parish, but I shall hope to make clear which is being discussed whenever the distinction is important.

The Domesday entry shows that the township was made up of three manors in 1066. The amount of land under the plough, four carucates, was about 450-500 acres. It could be worked by three ploughs (no doubt one to each manor).

After 1066, Ilbert de Laci, as overlord, allowed Gerneber to stay on. Gernber had three villeins and three bordars as tenants and they worked now only with two ploughs. No freemen are mentioned and no serf. The villeins and bordars had a social standing between the two.

Gerneber's household is not numbered nor are the families of his tenants, so that one can merely guess that between thirty and fifty people lived in Thornhill at that time. Gerneber held eleven manors in this district before 1066, of which he was allowed to keep four, but the value of his possessions dropped from about £11 to little more than £1 in 1086.

After 1086 we learn no more of Gerneber. No other documents which contain his name have been brought to light. Not until almost a century later does written historical evidence start the trickle which later becomes a flood.

---

(4) Shitlington comprises of Overton, Middlestown and Netherton. Euphemistically it was renamed Sitlington in the early years of the twentieth century.

Medieval Thornhill

Evidence from the twelfth century comes chiefly from charters which recorded changes in the holding of the land. From such charters we learn that two generations after Gerneber the name of one of the most important local landowners was Essolf (or Assolf). So extensive were his holdings that he gives the impression that he was a prototype of the Yorkshire business man, trading and then investing – necessarily in the land in those days – with considerable success. Since one of his grandsons bequeathed ironstone workings at Shitlington and Flockton to Rievaulx Abbey, perhaps Essolf had made money from such workings, for it was at a time when iron was being increasingly used for agricultural implements and certain instruments if war.

That is surmise, however; what we do know about him is that he had a large number of sons, amongst whom his holdings were eventually divided.

Some of his sons also appear to have been capable men, and one of them, Jordan, was constable of Wakefield (c. 1174-8) under Earl Warenne as overlord. A constable was in charge of the defence lord's establishments and in control of his forces should trouble break out. The Manor of Wakefield was very extensive, so that Jordan's job would carry power and influence. To him came Thornhill and other manors near Halifax. He is mentioned as Jordan de Tornil in some charters of the late twelfth century. Certainly two or three sons took the surname "de Thornhill", and from one of them the consequent genealogy of the family is traced with confidence.

Jordan interesting is the subject of one of the windows in Canterbury Cathedral. An account exists that was written shortly after the occurrence portrayed in the window. Two monks of Canterbury were writing about the miracles said to have been performed by St. Thomas of Canterbury after his death. The story includes much interesting detail and the following account is a very brief summary of it.[5]

> A band of pilgrim from Canterbury arrived at Jordan's House at a time when his household had been attacked by disease, and his son William, was laid for burial. With the aid of pilgrims' water, in which a drop of the Saint's blood had been mixed, the boy was restored life. but Jordan delayed the performance of his vow to make a pilgrimage to Canterbury. Another son, older than William and more beloved – "because his father's race was showing in his features", was seized with a violent illness. Then the vow was preformed; and the knight and his wife, ill themselves almost to the point of death, journeyed to Canterbury with the body whose life they owed to the miraculous power of St. Thomas.

Nine scenes from the legend fill the lower part of the sixth window on the north side of the Chapel of St. Thomas in Canterbury Cathedral. The glass dates from the early part of the thirteenth century. The features, gestures, and expressions of the various figures are rendered with great skill.

The Thornhill family in 1165 had a very modest fortune, but gradually they built up more extensive holdings – helped by careful marriages as the medieval custom was – and in the early fourteenth century Sir John de Thornhill and his wife Beatrice were owners of large

---

(5) This shortened account, and some of the other information of this period is taken from "The Thornhill Family" by C.T. Clay, in the *Yorkshire Archaeological Journal*. Vol 29.

3. Jordan, son of Essolf, performing his vow at the Shrine of St. Thomas in Trinity Chapel, Canterbury Cathedral. (V & A)

parts of the Thornhill-Halifax area and parts of Lincolnshire. It was this Sir John (*c.*1260-1322) who obtained from the King in 1317 a charter permitting a weekly market and a yearly fair to be held in Thornhill.

Besides being of use to the villages such medieval markets and fairs were sources of income to the lord of the manor. He levied tolls at them; and it is an indication of Sir John's growing importance as well as the growth of the village that he was able to obtain this perquisite. The stump of the market cross still stands, though the weekly market has long since disappeared, but the fair in a truncated form carried on until quite recently as Thornhill Feast, continuous for over 600 years.

Sir John's heir, Sir Brian, had much power and influence in the whole country – not just the West Riding. He was at different times commissioner of array for the army, collector of subsidies (taxes), escheator (dealing in land forfeiture) and sheriff. In 1351, 1355 and 1358 he was knight of the Shire for Yorkshire in Parliament. An account exists which shows that as an MP he got expenses of £6 for 30 days – a rate of 4*s.* a day. That was at a time when a gallon of red wine cost 4*d.*

The later middle years

In the twelfth and thirteenth centuries the population of England increased rapidly, but feudalism persisted tenaciously in the social system. However, a great change in circumstances was coming. In 1348 and twice later in the fourteenth century, the Black Death caused tragic loss of life. The country's population was reduced by about a third by the epidemics. Actually the rate of increase of population had shown noticeable signs of falling off even before the plague hit the country, so that by the second half of the century the numbers left working on the land were considerably smaller than at the beginning of the century. This had the effect of hastening the disappearance of the feudal system. Peasants who had been tied to the land of their lord got greater freedom. Increasingly the lords' own demesne lands were leased to the more enterprising of their tenants, otherwise there was no one to till them. The growth of a yeoman class began.

Most men worked on the land in those days, of course, but there was some specialisation in other activities and crafts which inevitably increased with population increase. In hilly districts, which were not very suitable for the growing of crops, sheep were reared, and a great export trade to the continent grew up in wool, Yorkshire being well provided with hills, a source of almost unexpected wealth was open to this district.

Originally it was only on the continent that British wool was woven into cloth to any great extent, but no doubt some coarse cloth for home use was always made here, and as time went on, people took to manufacturing more than they needed themselves. Exports of wool dwindled and those of cloth increased. Again the West Riding of Yorkshire was favourably situated to join in the new trend. Its almost limitless supply of pure water from the hills could be used for washing and dying, and as a source of power for the primitive machinery used in fulling the cloth. In this way the West Riding textile industry was born.

In 1377, 1379 and 1381 poll taxes were levied throughout England to help pay for the disastrous wars against the Scots and the French. All adults over sixteen years of age were included, and lists were kept of their names and payments. The list in 1379 (still to be seen at the Public Record Office in London) is particularly interesting since it also mentions some special occupations.

Here are a few of the Thornhill entries:

(At this time it was stated that a quarter of wheat cost 4s., a gallon of white wine 6d., a gallon of red wine 4d.)

Joahannes Denay & Mary uxor ejus (his wife)	VI*d*.
- Souter (shoemaker)	VI*d*.
Alicia de Whitterley	IIII*d*.
Agnbes de Dewesom-Webster (weaver)	VI*d*.
Adam Waryn & Cecilia uxor ejus-Taillour	VI*d*.
Hugo Alaynson & Johanna uxor ejus-Naillour	VI*d*.
Willelmus King	IIII*d*.
Alicia Parker	IIII*d*.
Thomas Tyas & Alacia uxor ejus	IIII*d*.
etc., etc.	
summa	XXVJ*s*.VJ*d*.

Altogether 103 people are named but the poorest people did not pay, and some others found ways of eluding the tax. Also children are not in the list, so that it looks as if the total population of the township was perhaps 200-250 at that time. The total tax paid was 26*s*.6*d*. At the same time Whitley paid 6*s*. 10*d*., Flockton 11*s*. 4*d*., and Shitlington 18*s*. 2*d*. Dewsbury, still noticeably smaller than Thornhill, paid 14*s*.4*d*.

In the Thornhill list there are three weavers, whilst the Dewsbury one includes a merchant (who paid 1s.), a weaver, shearman and fuller - showing some textile activity at that early date. Note that the craftsmen (or women) paid more than the ordinary villager.

Throughout the whole of life - and in death - lord and tenants of a medieval manor were closely bound together. Besides the tenant owing services to the lord for his land he also came under his jurisdiction in day to day life. Severe infringement of the country's laws was treated by the travelling King's Justices or, after the fourteenth century, by local JPs at Quarter Sessions in the larger towns, but lesser offenses and misdemeanours were brought before the lord or his steward and (usually) a jury of villagers. Land transactions in the village were also dealt with in the local court. There manorial proceedings were carefully written down on rolls of parchment or vellum, with the result that quite a lot have survived to the present day.

The obligations of manorial life were not entirely in one direction. The lord had his, as well as the tenants, and although they were obviously far less restrictive in effect, he also, or his officers, could be involved in manorial jurisdiction. One of the examples below appears to show Sir John de Thornhill losing an argument about possession of a piece of land.

There are surviving Rolls from the Thornhill Manor Court dating from as early as 1303-5. Another set from 1348 are not in such good condition.

The following is a transcription of parts of the earlier ones. The fines were paid to the lord – a useful source of income for him.

Court held at Thornhill Wednesday in the week of Pentecost 31 Edward (1303)

Roger the miller acknowledges himself to be holden to Agnes Surkott in 16d. Therefore the said Agnes should recover the debt and the said Roger in mercy (*guilty, to be fined*) 6 hens,

Thomas son of the reeve claims against John Shephard that he defaulted in transferring 4 sheep in custody of the said John valued 3s. 2d. And the said John sought an enquiry and the said Thomas similarly to the next court.

William the reeve in mercy because he brewed contrary to the assize. And Agness Surcott similarly and the wife of Nicholas Bray similarly (*amount and strength of ale brewed was official fixed*).

Court of Thornhill Wednesday after the Translation of Thomas the Martyr in the said year.

William Foxholes in mercy for a beast taken in the lord's cornfield   6d.

Diana Graskes in mercy for a pig taken in the lord's park   6 hens.

Court of Thornhyll Wednesday on the Eve of St. Peter in Chains in same year.

Alice de Byttelay having a day assigned to prove whether Mikelforde was not in the custody of the lord came and showed a certain charter which testified that Henry the said Alice's husband and the said Alice were enfeoffed.

Two obvious points of interest in these entries are the method of dating according to the religious calendar and the use of hens for payment of fines. Notice, too, that it was a time of introduction of surnames. Some people are known by their father, some by their occupation, some by the district they came from, and some, apparently, by a surname proper.

Manorial courts persisted for centuries after the disappearance of other aspects of the old feudal system, but their powers gradually dwindled until they were little more than nominal.

A court of justice even older than the Manor Court was the "Sheriff Tourn". This was originally a meeting of the Wapentake (a collection of a hundred or so townships) presided over by the Sheriff. After the reign of Edward III, however, it was possible for a wealthy person to buy or lease the rights to hold the Sheriff Tourn – the Sheriff no longer having jurisdiction. This appears to have been done for the Wapentake of Agbrigg by the Saviles – holders of the Thornhill Manor after 1370 – and, although towards the end they appeared to do little apart from appoint a constable and a pindar, a jury called for a Sheriff Tourn met in Thornhill until the nineteenth century. The Tourn is recorded twice a year in the Vestry Book.

An account of a serious offense in Thornhill in the medieval period, roughly contemporaneous with the manorial offenses quoted above, can be found in the Assize Rolls for Yorkshire for 1293. The case was one of murder. An argument broke out between the parson of Dewsbury and the parson of Thornhill about certain of the Flockton tithes. The Dewsbury parson learned of this and sent off men of his to try to stop them. Fighting broke out and Henry de Thornhill fled to his parson's grange. He was followed and challenged to come out, whereupon:

> William of Dewsbury struck the aforesaid Henry with a certain sword in the middle of the body so that immediately he died thereof. And the aforesaid Edmund the Chamberlain, Robert the Cook and John Wyvel immediately after the deed conducted the aforesaid William of Dewsbury to the water of the Calder, and then led him back to the house of the aforesaid Thomas Coke, etc. And the aforesaid William of Dewsbury immediately after the deed fled, and is suspected. Therefore let him be summoned to appear or be outlawed. ...

Apparently William could not be found and he was outlawed at the suit of Henry's wife. The recourse to outlawing in those days (where the criminal was declared to be deprived of all protection of common law) shows up the inability of those concerned with the King's peace to track down and apprehend the man who fled. Whether the William in our story was ever found we do not know.

The Savile family

In 1370 the heir to the Thornhill estates was, for the first time, a woman – a child of two years old in fact. As an heiress Elizabeth was a considerable prize in the district, and in order to have the right to choose a husband for her Sir John Savile of Elland and Tankersley paid £126. 3s. 4d. to the King. The money would be worth three or four thousand pounds today.

Sir John married her to his second son, Henry. Descendants of theirs have held the estate until the present day – an unusually long time for land to stay in one family.

The history of the Savile family is one which includes many members of the unusual ability. From the fourteenth to the seventeenth centuries they appear to have been almost hereditary High Sheriffs of the country: they were MPs for Yorkshire, and in the seventeenth and eighteenth centuries two of them were politicians of the first rank. And besides there being branches of the family around Halifax and at Thornhill there were others at Lupset, Howley and Methley. In the sixteenth century Henry Savile of Bradley, Warden of Merton College, Oxford and Provost of Eton, was tutor in Greek to Queen Elizabeth I. He was a mathematician as well, and founder of the Savilian Chair of Geometry and Astronomy at Oxford. His brother John, who built Methley Hall, was the most famous lawyer of his day. Also in the sixteenth century Henry Savile of Lupset, commonly called "The Surveyor", was at sometime High Sheriff of Yorkshire, Surveyor of Crown Lands and member of the Council of the North. In the early seventeenth century Sir John Savile of Howley (originally an illegitimate branch of the Thornhill Saviles) was one of the founders of modern Leeds.

Thomas, son of Elizabeth de Thornhill and Henry Savile also became heir to the main Savile estates in Elland and Tankersley, and from then on Thornhill was the seat of the head of the family.

The Savile family chapel, built about 1447, is now, architecturally and historically, one of the most interesting parts of Thornhill Church. The oldest monument contained in the chapel is a stone figure of a knight in armour, probably Sir John de Thornhill who obtained the market and fair for the village. Other monuments include one of great curiosity made of oak and dated 1529. With effigies of Sir John Savile and his two wives it originally would have had an oak canopy over it, supported on four pillars and must have looked more like an old fashioned bedstead than a tomb. The inscription round it is

> "Bonys among stonys lye ful styl,
> quilst the sowle wanders whar God wyl"
> *Bones among stones lie full still whilst the soul wanders where God will.*

The stained glass in the chapel is medieval. With it and the great east window of the chancel Thornhill possesses one of the finest collections of medieval glass outside York. The east window of the chapel is dated 1498. Its subject is the Resurrection of the Dead. Small figures show, amongst other things, resurrected bodies leaving the tombs, St. Michael weighing the souls and St. Peter with the keys of the heavenly city.

The east window in the chancel is a Jesse window. It was put there in 1492 by Robert Frost, rector from 1482 to 1498. During the last war its glass was kept underground in Thornhill colliery to ensure that it survived. It cost £50 to take the glass out and £200 to put it back! Robert Frost was at one time Chancellor to Prince Arthur, Henry VII's eldest son.

4. The Savile Chapel. Built around 1477 and enlarged at the end of the century it contains many monuments and a Doom window. (GJ)

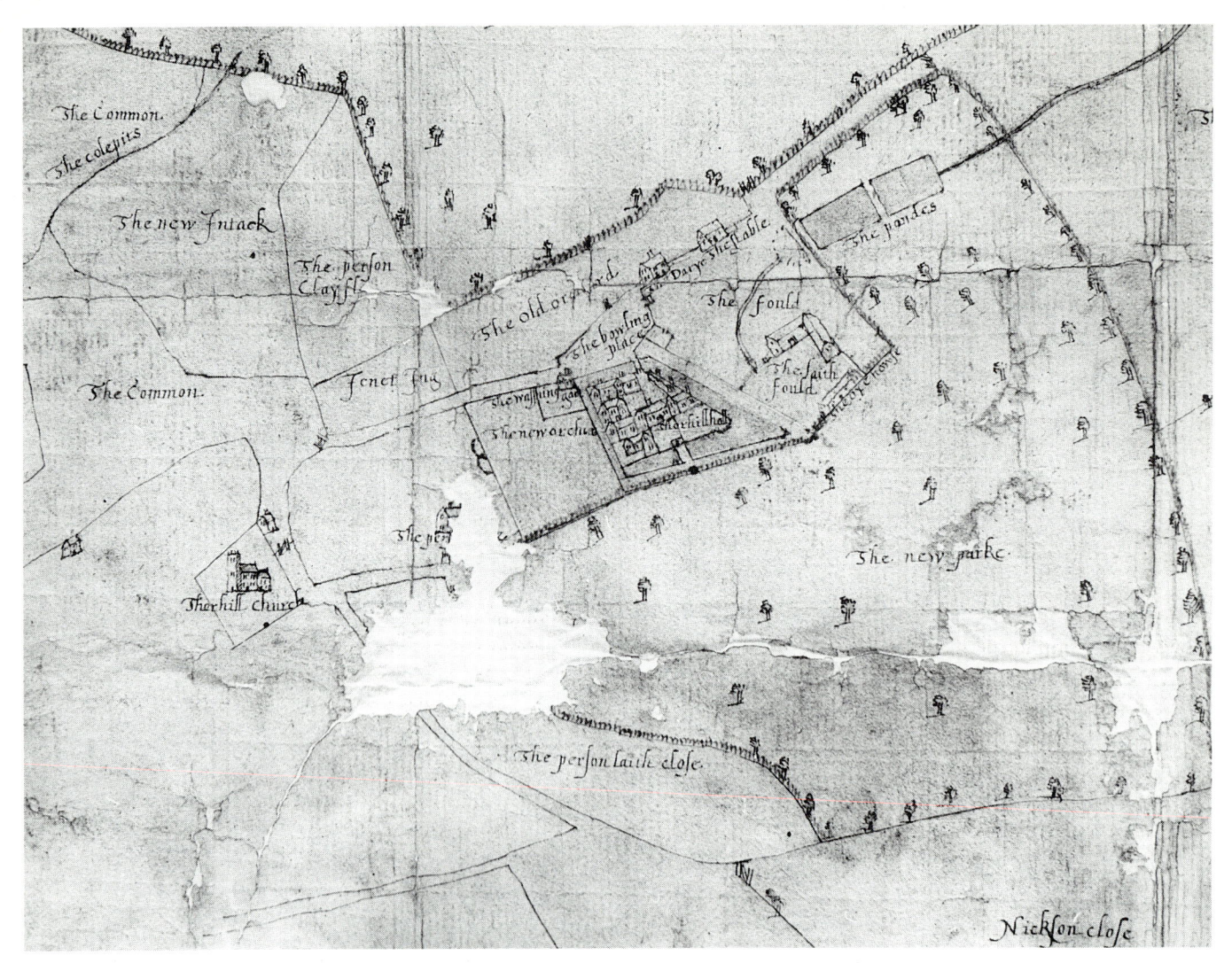

5. Thornhill Hall and Surroundings, 1602. Plan by William Saxton, ('Colepits' would be bell pits, 'Laithe' a barn, 'person' the parson). (NAS)

When Robert Frost was Rector his patron was Sir John Savile of the oak tomb. Sir John's second wife, Elizabeth Paston, was related to the royal family. This was the most splendid marriage of the earlier Saviles. Their son and heir, Henry, was an important almost notorious, character of the first half of the sixteenth century in Yorkshire. Like his forbears, he was High Sheriff of the county for several years. He steadfastly adhered to Henry VIII at the time of the Pilgrimage of Grace. He appears to have been a full-blooded, vigorous man with somewhat idiosyncratic ideas of right and wrong. It was he who started the illegitimate branch of the family which later lived at Howley Hall. He had two legitimate children and six illegitimate ones. The true heir, Edward, appears to have been simple-minded, and Henry left as much to the illegitimate heirs as he could. For many years the latter lived more splendidly than the Thornhill branch.

When Henry died he left something like 300 messuages, 300 tofts, 10 water mills, and 22,000 acres of land – not counting extensive wastes and commons.

Edward the Simple died without issue in 1604, and the Thornhill estates passed to the collateral branch of the family at Lupset.

Archaeological excavations on the site of the old Hall brought to light remains of a timbered building of about 1300 and of later stone buildings (of which two fragments remain) of about 1450 – the site being moated at this later date. The stone buildings date from just about the time that Thornhill became the home of the main branch of the Savile family. The excavations also indicate extensive alterations on the site about 1600: this was about the time that the estates passed to the Lupset branch.

The Lupset Saviles certainly re-invigorated the main branch. Sir George of Lupset and Thornhill, was married first to Lady Mary Talbot, daughter of the Earl of Shrewsbury and it was she who brought Rufford Abbey, Nottinghamshire, into the family, as dowry. Their son, George married Anne, a sister of Sir Thomas Wentworth, later Earl of Strafford – the famous Strafford who was executed in 1641 for his influence with Charles I. George died whilst his children were young and for some years his wife, Lady Anne, was in charge of the estates. During this time, in 1624, she had to deal with a situation which reads more like romantic fiction than fact.

The facts, though, can still be seen at York in the archives of the Consistory Court. The Revd Antony Binns, parson of High Hoyland, was brought before the Court for marrying in secret, at Thornhill Hall, without banns or licence, Thomas Edmonds of Wentworth Woodhouse (aged 27) and Anne Cookson (aged 20) – a gentleman's daughter who was probably one of Lady Anne's household. The young couple admitted to the court that Mr Binns had married them between 11 and 12 of the clock on a Sunday night. He had gone secretly into an inner court of the Hall and married them through the casement of a window – "through the casement of the chamber window where the said Anne Cookson laid".

The night of 7 March would probably have been cold and would certainly be dark, but the young people said they had no candles and the court tried to find out whether the service had been managed properly or not. Mr Binns knew the service by heart and whispered the words which they repeated after him. Anne said that the words repeated by her and her husband "were so spoken that they understood one another although they were spoken with a low voice". That was sufficient for the service to be binding.

In spite of the night's secrecy a rumour of what had happened was already abroad next morning – and Thomas Edmonds and Antony Binns were confronted by Charles Greenwood, Rector of Thornhill, as they stood talking together on the staircase leading to the Great Chamber. They seem to have made little effort to keep the secret any longer. Eventually Mr Binns was found guilty of having performed a clandestine marriage against the order of the church and without legal permission. He was suspended from clerical office. It is not known how long the suspension was to last – but when the case first came into court Thomas and Anne had taken the precaution of marrying again at Wentworth Woodhouse.

Sir George and Lady Anne Savile had a son William, born in 1612. William was a high-spirited impetuous and independent youth who, until he died in 1644, had an adventurous life fighting for the King. He married Anne, daughter of Lord Coventry, at Thornhill at the age of 17. His wife was a young woman of determination and resource who courage was clearly displayed in the troubled days of the Civil War. Their eldest son, George, afterwards the first and famous Marquis of Halifax, was a brilliant writer and statesman and a great favourite with Charles II because of his wit.

William was the nephew and (after his father's death) the ward of the Earl of Strafford. He was a strong supporter of his uncle and the royal cause, and when war broke out he was with the King at Nottingham at the raising of the Royal Standard. He soon gained distinction by his daring gallantry. One of his exploits in Yorkshire was to escape by swimming the River Aire when on the losing side in a battle at Leeds. In 1643 he was appointed governor of York, but he died there in January of the next year. He was buried at Thornhill, not quite 32 years old. His wife continued to work for the King's cause, and taking an active part in scheming and directing policy, she was at Pontefract Castle in 1648, the last place to hold out against the Parliamentarians. She helped clergy and others to escape the country. Amongst the Savile papers now held in Shire Hall, Nottingham, are several letters she wrote whilst her husband was alive. They contain little about politics or war, but for all that (perhaps even because of it) the impact they make is real and touching.

In one where she writes to "my Deare and Loving Husband Sir Wm. Savile" she asks about wall hangings (which kept some of the draughts out of their chill houses) wondering whether an old tent could be used as lining.

> I desired my uncle Hulton to entreate you to send word whether you would have yr. tent cutt to line hangings because they tell me it cannot be cut but with a great deale of losse by reason of ye deapth and many sloape seames

6. Lady Anne Savile, wife of Sir William Savile (3rd Baronet), and mother of George, first Marquis of Halifax. (LS, KMC)

in it. I have reprieved it hitherto in hope till to know yr. further pleasure concerning it.

In another she speaks of their son who became the first Marquis of Halifax. At the time he was about seven years old, and must have been staying with his father in London.

> I am glad to hear George is well and I finde by

yr. letter you sent mee hee is in great liklyhood to prove a scholler wch. I think would please you very well I pray god bless him and make him an honest man however.

Sir William's hope were more than justified and Lady Anne would not have been altogether disappointed in hers. For a politician George was more honest than many.

Apologising for its length, Lady Anne ends another letter-

> I have now proved Nan ye long scribler but I know it is in errour you will pardon in yr. loving wife –   A Savile.

These simple letters which have lain unopened for over 300 years, have more flavour of the period and people (to the writer of this booklet at least) than any collection of facts and lists of events.

Thornhill in 1634

A map of Thornhill was made for Sir William Savile in 1634; it is in excellent condition.

The Calder, which twists and then bends sharply, is shown as the boundary of "The Lordship of Thornell" to the north and east. To the south is a wandering stream and along its length is written "This beck is called Smithie Brook". There are other names recognisable to present day inhabitants of Thornhill: "near Hostingley", "Ludwell Field", "The Boot", "Soyles Close" and a large empty tract of land called "Leys Moor". At the bend of the river where it is nearest to Dewsbury (but quite separated from it there, as there is no bridge across at that date) is field shown as "Town Close". This may have been one allowed for the common use of the villagers. It is certainly the part known as Savile Town today.

The map also shows the Hall surrounded by the moat in the "New Park" and the "Great Park" which stretched as far as the river in the direction of Earlsheaton. The church is there of course, and the Old Rectory. The old Rectory was, in fact, twice rebuilt after that date, but on the same site and each time incorporating a little of the Elizabethan building on the east side. The two houses at opposite corners of the churchyard (one of them now the Savile Arms) are plainly marked, and so are many of the farms which still flourish, but most of the houses obviously clustered along the road still known as The Town. They all have a small parcel of land attached the "toft and croft" of medieval times obviously still surviving.

Especially to be noted are the three large areas called "Kirkenfield", "Ludwell Field", and "Ash Furshott", Divided from one another by the Town, Frank Lane, and Edge Lane, they are considerably larger than the "closes" around them and, fairly clearly, are remnants of the medieval system of arable farming – the "Common Field" or "Strip" system. The closes, from their long and narrow shapes, must have been formed from strips which were originally parts of these fields. There is a fourth area, "Northcliffe Field" at Edge Top, beyond what is now the Black Horse Inn – but probably because of its bleak position, it appears to have been of little interest to individual farmers for closes and may, by that time, only have been used as pasture land.

The map is coloured and there are wonderful birds and beasts in the parks being shot at by sportsmen dressed, of course, in the elaborate costume of the time. Another man is shown fishing in the Calder. The map was made for the "Right Worshipful Sr. William Savell Knight and Baronett by his servant Edw. Rolsonn".

Besides being lively and brave, Sir William inspired at least one friend to compose Latin verses about him. The poet is kept anonymous, but the verses are quoted in *Loidis & Elmete* written by T D Whitaker in 1816. They give an idea of Christmas festivities at the Hall before the troubles of the Civil War, and of the life led by gentlemen of those days.

Here are the most interesting parts:

> ... your house is filled with guests from near at

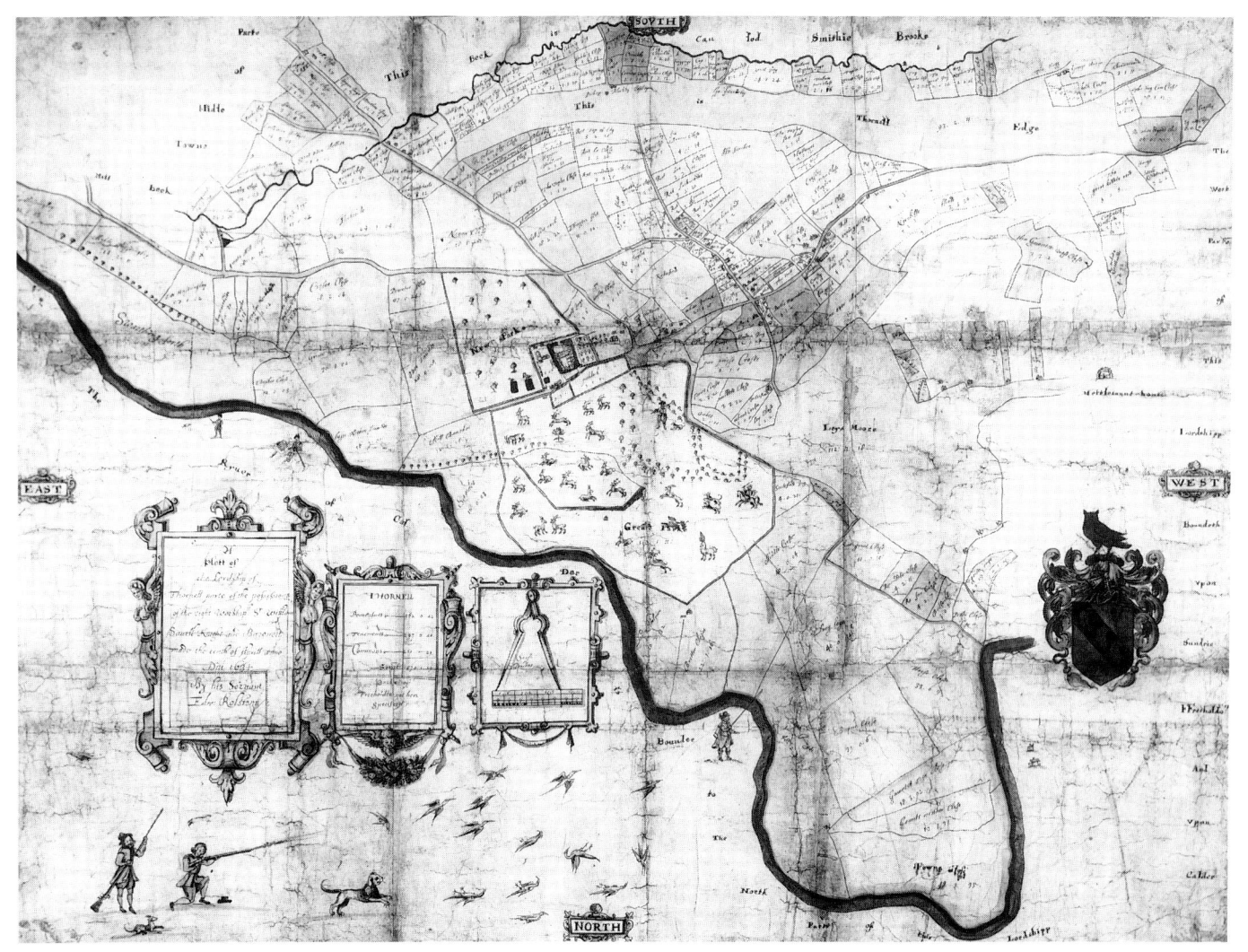

7. Thornhill in 1634. Note that North – Dewsbury direction – is at the lower edge of the plan. (LS, KMC)

hand and resounds with varied talk ... the rafters ring with many a peal of laughter, while the coal is glowing and the jar pours forth its raisins. ... The bread pan glows hot under the minced meat pies, while swine's neck with mustard and saddle of ox ... many a goose and a swan here and there adorn the table. ... It pleased us to mix wit with wine and to laugh without restraint at the jests of those call for more.

Further verses are written in a different mood:

> Not now as formerly does it please me to cling ... to the horses back while the hounds follow the tricky course of a hare, with keen scented nose. ... I play a hand of cards and without luck beguile the day ... in hoping for a change in the run of the dice. ... So long as I may touch the tight strings of the lute with flashing hand and sound a strain worthy of Savile's ears, I do not envy you your bounteous Table, your dances and your tightly laced maidens.

Though they were not nearly as wealthy as the Saviles, by the end of the sixteenth century two or three other families of note were to be found in Thornhill – the Nettletons, Elmsalls, and Radcliffes.

The Nettletons lived at Lees Hall, a half-timbered house dating from about 1420. Part of the original house still stands. Its survival is due to the extraordinary efforts of Mr Reginald Mortimer who farms the adjoining land. At one time the house was in such a neglected and ruined state that it looked as though nothing could save it, but Mr Mortimer has spent years of effort at his own expense in rescuing and restoring it as much as possible. Its surroundings are not what they once were; it stands these days in the shadow of pit dumps and water cooling towers, but that so much of a half-timbered house of that age has survived in this district is quite remarkable.

The Radcliffes lived at Overthorpe Hall. Sir George Radcliffe was lawyer assistant and eventually great personal friend to the Earl of Strafford. He was imprisoned at different times because of this, and finally, during the Commonwealth, had to leave the country. A book of his letters exists which shows that whatever the faults of either men, he like Strafford, had a very strong sense of duty and personal loyalty. This trait shows up clearly even in the letters he wrote as a boy. Some of the most interesting of the collection – written to "his deere and lovinge Mother at Overthorpe, Thornhill" – give glimpses of his young days at a boarding school in Oldham and, later, his life at University College, Oxford.

When Strafford was awaiting death he wrote to George Radcliffe, as if to his very best friend.

> Gentle George, let me have your prayers to God for the forgiveness of my sinns and saving of my soule. Meete I trust we shall in Heaven, but I doubt not on earthe. Howbeit, all men living I should be gladest to spend an hour with you privately; if that might be admitted, that might be a comfort to me; to see you at a distance but a trouble and disturbance.

The letter is dated "Sunday morning, 9th May". Strafford was executed on the twelfth.

The Elmsalls were probably yeoman farmers until well into the seventeenth century, but in the early eighteenth century William Elmsall was a lawyer of note and his son Henry was Rector of Thornhill from 1732 to 1759. A diary kept by William between 1708 and his death in 1740 was found in London and deposited in Sheffield City Library. It has been described as unique because it gives a day by day account of legal business in the eighteenth century. It shows too, that Mr Elmsall travelled up to 200 miles a week on horseback in the course of his duties and, that being so, not surprisingly, the weather also figures daily in the diary. In January 1739/40 he wrote (presumably about the Calder) "River so frozen that wheel carriage drives on the ice".

The Civil War

Following the death of Sir William Savile, as mentioned above, Lady Anne continued to work and intrigue for the Royalist cause, Every trick of the Parliamentarians to try to trap her she eluded, and she continued to give help and money to the clergy and distressed cavaliers.

Pontefract was the last refuge of Royalist resistance. It withstood a siege by the Parliamentarians until two months after the execution of Charles I. During the siege the Parliamentarians decided that the garrison at Thornhill must be reduced. Lady Savile was not there (we do not know her exact whereabouts) but she was supporting the Royalists in Pontefract with arms and horses. Accordingly, a body of men under Colonel Charles Fairfax, detached from those advancing on Pontefract, was sent to take possession of Thornhill Hall.

An account of what happened is given in a letter written by Fairfax himself and dated "Thornhill, 22nd July, 1648". The garrison could not have been large, but it is quite clear from the extra help Fairfax needed that it put up expected resistance.

The letter begins:

> Sir, being ordered with about 500 of my Regiment of foot accompanied with 200 of Colonel Sir Henry Cholmley's horse to march to Thornhill Garrison, I intended to have been there last Saturday night, but too much of that day was spent in pacification of the soldiers, that exclaimed for pay: (and indeed they are gallant men, if they were not too clamorous). It was past nine next morning before we came thither. We possessed ourselves of the church and Parsonage House (a stone cast from the Hall), without opposition, sent them the summons to which we have these answers and replies here enclosed.

From Colonel Fairfax to Thomas Paulden, Governor of Thornhill Hall:

> Sir, – We thirst after no man's blood, but desire that God will scatter the people that delight in warre. I doe therefore as here commanded for settlement of these parts, and prevention of insurrection and tumults demand of you the hold, wherein you now are, together with your armes to be forthwith delivered into my hands for the use of the King and Parliament. If this motion be rejected, expect hostilities, and the Lord look upon each of us according to the sincerity of his heart, as we desire our peace to the greatest honor both of God and King.

Thornhill: 16th July, 1648.   C Fairfax

From Thos Paulden to Colonel Fairfax, Commander-in-Chief, of Thornhill Town

> Sir – In answer to your demands I return we are equally with you desirous to prevent Christian bloodshed. But to your demand of the house we answer that we may not part with our loyalty, but together with our blood: we were commanded hither by our lawful superiors and may not in honor or duty part hence without their order. But if you please to suffer a messenger from us to go to the Governor of Pontefract Castle, at his return you may expect to have a further answer from, sir, your servant.
>
> Thomas Paulden

A further letter from Fairfax only elicits the reply:

Reply from Thos. Paulden to Col Fairfax

> Sir, you may not expect anything here, but what you can win with your sword, until I receive further commands from my superiors – Yours, Thos. Paulden

Fairfax then continues with the story:

We intended that day (Sunday) only to take a view, but it proved an engagement. Very opportunely came to our assistance four troops of horse and two of dragoons, sent by Lieutenant-General Cromwell. We fell on the work, entered the barns, stables and malt house within the fold but without the moat. It was a very sharp dispute betwixt one and six. We spent most of our ammunition, viz., four barrels of powder, and sent presently to York and Leeds for more. We have about 12 slain men and 30 wounded, whereof a few of them mortally.

On Monday we cut off their fresh waters, then set workmen to draw off the moat, and on Tuesday towards night completed the work. Sir Henry Cholmley then came to us and we sent them this last summons.

Because of the overwhelming odds against them, no doubt, Paulden agrees on 18 July 1648 to a parley, asking that hostages shall be sent whilst this takes place.

Hostages were then appointed and Treators and we had a rendition upon articles to this purpose. That they should deliver to Sir Henry Cholmley and me the house and armes: only the Governor and Major Bonifant to have their horse and swords, as likewise a horse to one Jennings, a south countryman, who was one of the treators. They were to send us eleven of those Troopers my Lord General's Regiment surprised at the ferry, and the common soldiers only to march away with his apparel.

An hour before their march (which was seven at night) merely by accident the fire from their own party took hold of their powder, blew up part of the house, slew four or five of theirs, but none of our men, and miserably scorched about seven or eight more: and the same flame hath consumed all the buildings. I account it a mercy that it was done by themselves and cannot be objected against us. Some few armes the soldiers rescued but got little prize. The breach was on their part in not rendering the powder, but chiefly for that one of them took out a pistol, and many marched with their moneys: therefore it is confessed some lost their cloathes, for which cause the Governor and Bonifant refuse to send the eleven troopers, or render themselves prisoners according to engagement. Sir I cannot at present enlarge myself more than all humble respects to my noble good friends, being their and your servant.

Thornhill, 22nd July 1648   C Fairfax

So ended the old mansion, which had been the home of the Saviles for so many generations. Today, two small, ruined portions of it survive amongst a tangle of trees and undergrowth. The moat, which still makes an island of the site, is a delight for young boys who fish.

After the Civil War the Saviles made Rufford Abbey their main seat and so it remained until recently. After a boyhood at Thornhill, Sir William's son George, (later, Marquis of Halifax) was brought up at Rufford Abbey to the life of an opulent country gentleman. Politics, however, were to be his life interest and, as a member of the party known as the "Trimmers", he was Lord Privy Seal at sometimes during the reigns of three Kings; Charles II, James II and William III. He was also, for a time, Lord President of the Council. He died in 1695 and was buried in Westminster Abbey.

The present Lord Savile has returned to this district, living only about ten miles from the family's old home.

The villages and village life

Now we come to the part of our history when we are chiefly concerned with what happened in Thornhill after it had lost its close connection with its famous family. It would be useful, therefore, to see what we know of village life up to this point.

In the Middle Ages most Englishmen were peasant farmers, and in Thornhill, from the evidence of the map of 1634, it looks as if they followed the common field system of agriculture. In this system, one, two or even three fields were cropped and one left fallow, annually. The crops, which were rotated, were usually rye, wheat or oats and peas, beans or lentils. Each man would have a few strips in all three fields and an equivalent proportion of meadows in the lower-lying land. His animals would roam the commons (rough pasture) freely. As the years went by, however – as was happening in many parts of England – it looks as if some men found it more convenient to make exchanges, or buy, so that their land lay in one parcel in each field, then it could be enclosed.

Others in these Pennine-fringe areas must have found it more convenient to reduce their land-holdings and turn to the growing textile trade for a livelihood. But all would still have their croft where they could grow crops for their own use and keep a few animals.

Law and order was mostly a local affair. In medieval times it was taken care of in the Sheriff Tourn or Manorial Courts. As these decayed parish constables and local JPs took control, their power coming from the courts of Quarter Sessions. The centre for the organisation of village life also changed from the Lord's Hall to the vestry of the church. Officials and overseers were chosen from the villagers in turn. In the seventeenth century the main officials were the Churchwardens, the Constable and the Overseers of the Poor. They were joined in the eighteenth century by the Overseers of the Highways.

But in Thornhill manorial courts had quite a long life. They were still functioning usefully in the seventeenth century. This is clearly shown in the court rolls, some of which exist up to 1651. In addition, a roll for 1630 shows that a common-field system of agriculture still obtained for a number of villagers at that date even if some enclosure had already taken place.

Here are excerpts:

> **Thornhill: Court Baron** of Lade Anne Savile, widow, relict of Sir George Savile, Knight, deceased ... of the manor of Thornhill held there the second day of August in the sixth year of the reign of our Lord King Charles, etc. (1630).
>
> All the jurors say upon their oath that Henry Scholefield did not make a certain portion of the hedge in the Hardcornfield as he was laid in pain to, whereas he is in the lord's mercy ... 12*d*.
>
> Also they say that Humus Burdett gent. did not make a certain portion of the hedge in the aforesaid field wherefore he is in the lord's mercy ... 3*s*. 4*d*.

The Hardcornfield was one of the three fields which was sown with winter corn – a mixture of rye and wheat. The hedges were temporary ones, probably of brushwood, which were taken down again after the harvest so that animals could graze the stubble freely.

8. View across the moat to the site of the old Thornhill in c.1910. The white stone figures of Gog and Magog were put in there in the nineteenth century. (KCS/S/0561)

9. Remains of Thornhill Hall, April 1995. (GJ)

Note that Humus Burdett, gent. pays considerably more than plain Henry Scholefield for a similar offense. And Humus Burdett was in fact, one of the two "affeerors" (assessors of fines) of the court that day.

Another roll which has survived from 1581 shows the manor court treating offenses against the Queen's Peace.

> The jurors present on their oath that Robert Lawe made assault and affray upon John Allan and Lawrence Allan against the peace and that he shed blood from each of them against the said peace of the Lady Queen wherefore the aforesaid Robert Lawe is in the Lord's mercy ... 10s.
>
> And that Robert Lawe on the 29th October in the above year, about the seventh hour after noon of the same day, made assault and affray upon Thomas Hamshawe and drew blood from the same. Thomas against the peace of the Lady Queen wherefore he is in the Lord's mercy. 10s. And likewise the aforesaid jurors say that the aforesaid Robert Lawe made affray upon John Beaumonte after the last court and threatened the same John from time to time so that he could not go about his work, wherefore the same Robert Lawe is in the lord's mercy ... 3s. 4d.

A pugnacious, even bloodthirsty, character.

The church had a significant influence on the villagers' lives. Certainly until the Reformation its disciplines and its yearly procession of festivals would be a strong unifying force in the community, for everyone took part in them. The parson and the churchwardens were the disseminators of social conscience and social welfare. Social welfare depended on the church or private benevolence until the end of Queen Elizabeth's reign. Then the country recognised by law the responsibility of more fortunate men to subscribe to the poor. Local Overseers of the Poor had to be appointed and they were given powers to levy a local rate.

A church in Thornhill dates, as we have said, from before the Conquest. Its living was never appropriated by monastery or lay rector as happened to so many churches in the Middle Ages. In 1292 it was valued at £40 a year – a very considerable amount indeed for those days – and in the seventeenth century at £300. It is easy to see that it was desirable living and this would, no doubt, greatly enhance the selection of people from whom the lords of the manor could choose their rectors. They appear, usually, to have chosen wisely through many centuries. The list of Rector's names now to be seen on a board at the back of the church is certainly a list of very able men, and what can be surmised of their conscientiousness is usually to their advantage.

As mentioned previously, Robert Frost, Chancellor to King Henry VII's eldest son, had the living in the fifteenth century. It was a time of pluralities in the livings and at the same time Robert Frost was also Archdeacon of Winchester, but since he put in the great east window, clerestoried and arched the chancel and built the south chapel, he could not be accused of neglecting Thornhill church.

During the Commonwealth the non-conformist minister who held it was Joshua Witton, who had been Fairfax's chaplain. Witton had to face keen questioning from a friend about his willingness to receive so much money, but there is no doubt from his later history (after he was replaced at Thornhill because he refused to subscribe to the Act of Uniformity) that he, too, was a man greatly valued by his friends for his judgement and honesty.

After the Reformation no doubt the power of the church declined, but as late as 1764 the rector of the day reported no dissenters – a striking testimony, at that date, to the satisfaction and unity of his flock.

Any education the village could offer before the seventeenth century probably also depended on the church, but we know nothing of how it might have been carried on. In 1619 Tobias Drake was given a licence to teach, but where or what he taught we cannot say. However, when Charles Greenwood, Rector, died in 1642 he left

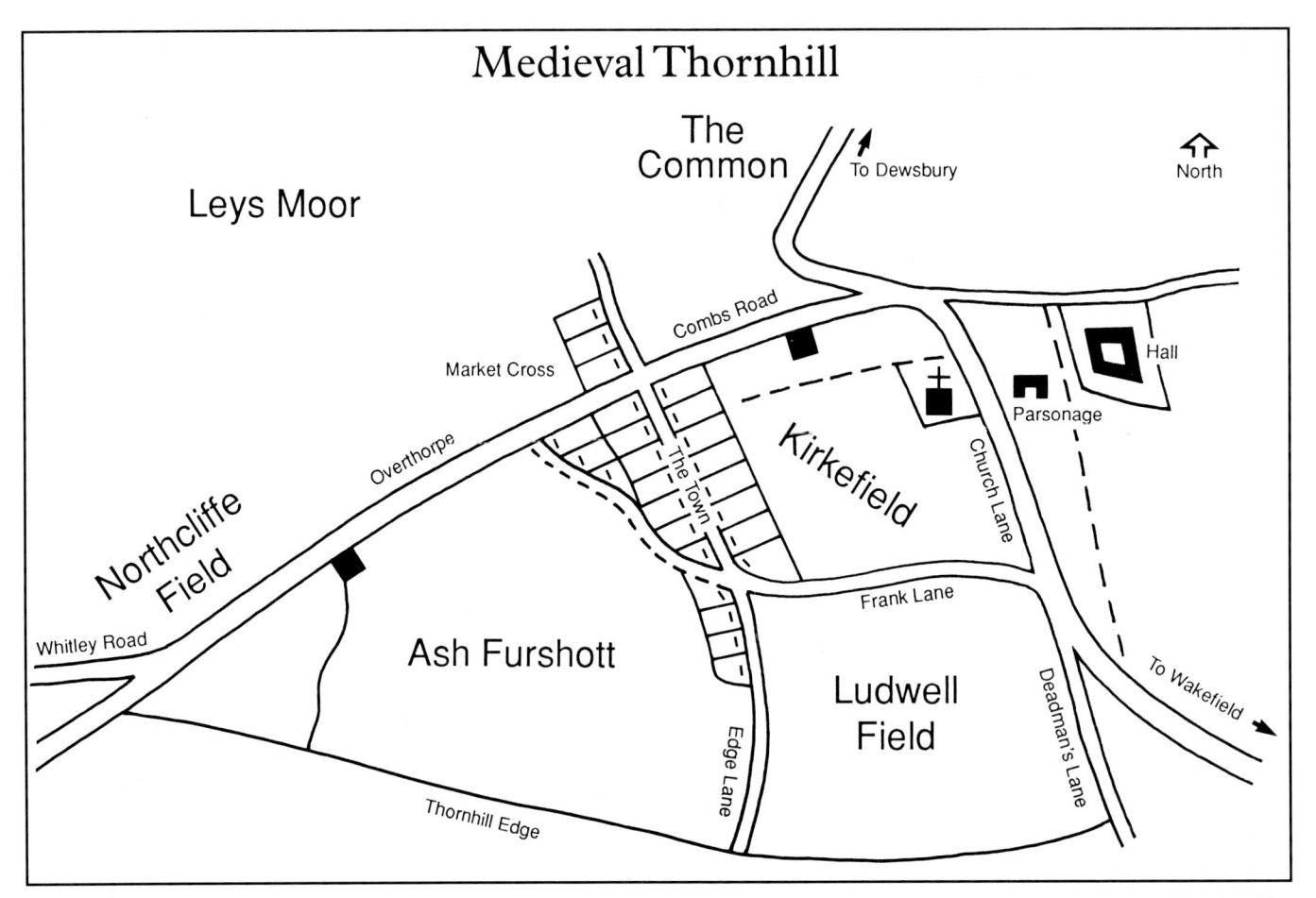

10. Medieval Thornhill. There were almost certainly great common fields in Thornhill in medieval times (indicated in this sketch) where villagers farmed in intermingled strips. Most of the houses, each with a croft, flanked "The Town".
(LS WYAS)

money in his will for the endowing of a Grammar School in the township. The endowment was a considerable one – £500. £250 was to be spent on a school house, and the rest was to give a salary of £20 a year to the schoolmaster. For those days it was a distinctly generous salary and, as such, it is interesting to compare it with the £300 the rectors received.

The school taught poorer local boys free of charge. Amongst the Savile papers are some which give accounts of the money spent on the free scholars in the year 1669. Mr Richard Wilson was schoolmaster: Thomas Pollard was tailor for them, and Mr John Clough was mercer. It cost 2s. a week each for their "table". Sadly, one of the boys died. The accounts on his behalf read:

Surgeon	£1. 1.0
Coroner	13.4
Winding sheet	3.3
Cakes and Ale at his funeral	12.6

For the seventeenth century we have the names of at least six boys who went from Thornhill Grammar School to Cambridge University.

In 1666 the government subjected all householders except the poorest to a "Hearth Tax". On each hearth in their houses they were taxed one shilling. From this tax we can get a rough idea of the size of the houses of the period, remembering that the total number of rooms would probably be of the order of twice the number that had fireplaces.

There is no indication of how many people in Thornhill were too poor to pay but fifty-seven people in all did pay, Mr Radcliffe (of Overthorpe Hall) and Doctor Lacy (the Rector) had the largest houses with nine hearths each. Twenty-eight people had two or more (up to seven).

This is quite a high standard of housing with an average noticeably higher than the rest of the parish (Shitlington, Flockton, Whitley) but about the same as Dewsbury's. However, although the average standard of housing was about the same, ninety-one people paid the tax in Dewsbury. In population it had, apparently, now overtaken Thornhill.

Reviewing the situation then, Thornhill in the seventeenth century was still only roughly the same size as it had been in 1379. Its inhabitants would all have their own small piece of land around their own homes, but a number of them by this time must have given up farming on a large scale to get a living by undertaking one or more processes in the home manufacturing of woollen cloth. Some of the less fortunate or less able ones who had not enough land for subsistence farming and who failed to succeed in the textile trade would have become casual labourers, but the number of poor was probably not great. There was a fair sprinkling of the yeoman class and a few gentlemen farmers. The church must have had a noticeable influence on the corporate life and education was probably somewhat above average for a place of such a size because of that influence. Certainly it was above average after the grammar school was endowed – but there must always have been a fair proportion of the villagers who received little or no formal schooling.

Until the end of the sixteenth century the greatest part of what we know about our village stems from the concerns of its two big land-owning families of Thornhill and Savile. We learn of other inhabitants at intervals – when taxation was recorded, in occasional land transactions or brushes with the law – but after 1580 another important source of knowledge becomes available. The villagers at last emerge from their anonymity: for, in that year, the parish registers were started.

The Parish Registers

It became compulsory to keep a record of births, marriages, and deaths in England in 1538, but in many cases the earlier ones appear to have been written on separate sheets of parchment or paper and, consequently, have disappeared. The Thornhill records start in 1580. The writing of the earliest books is very difficult to read, but all the entries up to the early nineteenth century have been carefully copied and reprinted in modern type. The spelling was left by the transcribers as it is in the original entries.

The entries refer to Thornhill, Flockton, Shitlington, (Overton, Middlestown and Netherton) and Whitley with Briestfield.

In 1580 there are twenty-six entries in all (14 christenings, 2 marriages, 10 burials). In 1599: sixty entries (36 christenings, 6 marriages, 18 burials).

Compare those with 1800 when there are 192 entries (99, 37 and 56) or 1801 with 222 entries (150, 19 and 53).

In 1801 the first census was taken and the population was given as:

Thornhill	1,499
Flockton	800
Shitlington	1,166
Whitley	819

a total of 4,284 in the parish.

Comparing this with register entries gives a method of getting a very rough estimate of population at any previous time. In this was it would seem that the population of Thornhill alone during the seventeenth century was probably around 400-500 out of about 1,200-1,500 in the parish.

Using statistical methods, parish registers are being increasingly studied these days to find out details about the sixteenth, seventeenth and eighteenth centuries that were once thought impossible to know. The registers must have been well kept and have few missing years: Thornhill's are in this category. The monthly totals of all baptisms, marriages and burials at Thornhill, between 1590 and 1813 have been sent to Cambridge University to add to similar figures from other places all over England for purposes of comparative study – and large scale graphs of the Thornhill figures show quite vividly the variations in these vital statistics over the centuries. The results of these investigations cannot, of course, be as accurate as those of a modern census but they can still be valuable and worthwhile. With particularly suitable registers – and much more intensive work! – it is possible to work out detailed lists of families in a village over a number of years – to see how big was the average family, to find out the average age at marriage and death (even though these are not stated in the register) and for example to find how far people were prepared to travel for a job or to find a wife. It has been deduced from figures already studied, that, in some parts of England at least, towards the end of the seventeenth century there was a period when there appears to have been conscious family limitation. This is a most unusual feature to find before the nineteenth, or even twentieth century, and it raises fascinating questions of why and how.

But the most interesting thing about the registers of one's own village is reading them as they stand. Here are some excerpts from Thornhill's:

A Register in the yeare of our Lord God 1582

John Robucke and Jenet Haule was maryed the 8 day of Julye.

John Otes had a child buried the 13 day of October.

Robert brodley had a child chrisned the 24 day of October named Agnes.

Margaret Robinsone had child chrisned the 20 day of January named John base begotten Richard Tayller she sayth is father to it.

A Regester 1587

John Aline and Alse hurste was maryed the xxij of Auguste.

ould Justice wyfe of the new hall was buryed the vj day of September.

John Beatsone was buried xxix of September.

John Beatsone wife was buried ij of October.

1606	A child wch. was bass begotten and wheare borne at the cole pits named Ann the XVIII of Jan.
1633	Ladie Ann the relict of Sir George Savile late of Thornhill Knight died the 30th of July between the houres of 6 and 7 in the afternoon and buried the 31st of July, 1633.
1673	George, the son of John Firth of Barkisland being one of the Hospitall boyes was buried the 9th day of July.
1699	Sept 7 Isaac Crowder a poor Boy being slaine in a coale Pitt at Flockton was buried.
1718	Eliz. Briggs of Thornhill – Excommunicated.

In the seventeenth century, in an effort to bolster the native woollen trade it became an offense to have a shroud made of anything except woollen industry wool, and in 1678 we find the affidavit being sworn that

> Robert Huntingdon of the parish of Thornhill, aforesaid lately deceased, was not put in wrapt or wound up or buried in any shirt, shift, sheet or shroud, made or mingled with Flax, Hempe, Silke, Haire, Gold or Silver; or other then wt. was made of sheeps woole only, not in any coffin lin'd or faced with any cloth stuff or any other thing whosoever made or mingled with Flax, Hempe, Silke, Haire, Gold or Silver or any other material but sheeps wool only.

Between 1665 and 1706 an account was kept of collections which had been ordered by official "briefs". As can be seen, people's charitable impulses were directed far and wide.

1665	Given the 21 day of May towards the reliefe of John Bedford of Emley the some of one shilling sixpence	0 1 6
1666	Maye the 27 Colected at Thornhill towards the relief of the towne of Hartlepoole in the county of durham the sum of five shillings fourpence	0 5 4
1671	May Collected towards the reliefe of the poor prisoners taken captive by the Turks the some of	2 13 6
1673	Sept; ye 21st Collected at Thornhill towards the losses done by fire beginning in ye Theatre Royall in London the some of	0 19 6

(?1680) The names of those of those that have contributed within ye Parish of Thornhill towards the building of St. Paules in London.

There are 47 names and they include:

Mr Savile, Rector	3	0	0
Mrs Nettleton	0	5	0
Rob Hepworth	0	0	2
Widw Scargill	0	0	1
Richard Pollard	0	0	1

and altogether their total was over £5.

Then:

Fockton's part	0	5	1
Whitley and Briestwell	0	2	11
Nether Shitlington	0	5	4
Over Shitlington	0	2	8

so that the whole parish sent   6   0   5

(?1680) towards the redeeming of the Captive Slaves of Algears   3   0   11

1681   March ye 5th Collected for ye Protestant Churches in the lesser Poland   0   8   7

1696   Sept. 6th Aby Lincolne   0   3   4

1703/4   5th March for ye poor distressed inhabitants of Orange who were forced out of their country by the French King the sum of   1   5   6

1705   25th March. South Molton Devon   0   6   1

1705   5th April. Collected Towards ye sufferers by ye Great Wind which happned in November 1703   1   2   11

Throughout the registers to 1812 the names which occur most frequently amongst Thornhill people include Armitage, Beaumont, Bedford, Blackburn Brooke, Dixon, Fisher, Haigh, Hampshire, Hepworth, Jackson, Kay, Lee, Pollard, Senior, Sykes, Taylor, Walker, White, Wilcock and Wood. They are still amongst the most frequent names here today.

The Vestry Accounts

The registers give us the names of the villagers and information about their baptism, marriage and death, but there are also in church two very large books which tell us something of their day-to-day affairs. These are the Vestry Accounts, and they extend from 1672 until after 1800, spanning the whole of the eighteenth century. They include accounts from all the main village officials previously mentioned – Churchwardens, Constable, Overseers of the Poor and (after 1720) Overseers of the Highways. Some discussion of the financial aspects of the accounts is made in a later section. This one is given up to showing a very small fraction of the interesting details of the entries.

From the Churchwarden's Accounts

£ s. d.

An account of Thornhill clock wch was bought into church and set up the 24th day of March 1675.

To Christofer Walton for the clock making 6 0 0

To John Townend for Boards for the case 1 16 8

To William Stephenson for the same making and nails and other necessaries 0 18 0

Charges in suite for not paying for the boards in time 0 12 0

Total charge 9 6 8

That for looking to and oyling the clock, for ringing five in the morning and eight of the clock at night daily – for ringing on Sundayes a peal of a quarter of an hour long at least and chime afterwards, for ringing on the 5th November and the 29th of May – for oyling the bells and finding rope for ye clock and bells, is to be paid three pounds by quarterly payment 3 10 0

1689 For a new church Bible 1 4 0
For three Communion plates 0 4 6

1699 For 6 gallons of wine when ye Bishop came to confirme at Thornhill 1 16 0

1708 For an otterhead and 2 Foomards 0 1 8

1716 For ye dog-whipper and for ye church sweeping (for a year) 0 18 0

To ye ringers of ye King's Coronation Day 0 3 0

For 3 New Bell wheels, a New Brass for Iron work and for clappers mending 7 0 0

1749	Charge upon Parson, curate and Clerk Aug 6 For Dinner	0 3 4	
Sept 3	For their Dinners etc	0 3 4	
Oct 7	For their Dinners and Ale	0 3 4	
Nov 5	For their Dinners and Ale (and on other occasions)	0 3 4	

1823	To 59 Hedgehogs and Polecats	14 9
	965 Sparrows	1 8 6
		2 3 3

Note the money for vermin destroyed – and the effect of giving 3s. to the bell-ringers of 1716.

The Constable's Accounts

1675	March 19. Charges upon a sick woman with two small children going towards Lincolnshire 4d. and for carrying them to the Constable of Horberry 12d. in all	0 1 4
1688	In ale to ye people that watched on ye nights being 11 nights each man 2d.	0 12 10
	For 3 quarters of gun powder to ye watch	0 0 9
1698	June 3. An assessment made by vertue of An Act of Parliament for granting to his Majestie ye sum of £1,484,015.1s. 11¾d. for disbanding forces paying seamen etc. This town's proportion being	55 4 9
1706	Charges when we set Jos. Pool in ye stocks	0 0 6
1707	A warrant for ye Cloth-searcher and my charges	0 2 0
	For ye commons driving	0 2 0
	For going the monthly search	0 4 0
1712	For ye Stocks and Cuckstoole mending	0 2 6
1745	Charges for ye first Watch House building	0 3 6
	For wood for ye Watch House	0 16 3
	For 2 Coale baskets etc. etc.	0 0 6
	Paid to Nine Teams going to Leeds with soldier's baggage	6 15 0

Poor people passing through a district were helped on their way (sometimes forcibly) and given a small dole. Note the old forms of punishment still prepared for with stocks and ducking-stool; the tax levied (to farthings!) by William of Orange's government to pay for war; the "cloth-searching" to guard against sharp practices by clothiers and, finally, preparation against revolution in 1688 and the "Young Pretender" in 1745.

Overseers of the Poor Accounts

These accounts are very long. They include many sad case histories; two of the fuller ones are quoted.

| 1691 | Charges about ye Buriall of Tripping Mary | 0 | 12 | 6 |

1721 This order following was agreed by the inhabitants of Thornhill at a meeting on Wednesday 29th November 1721.

That every person who requires Reliefe of the Towne and to enter into weekly pay shall have the Poor Badge set upon his or her Clothes by the Overseers of the Poor for the time being and the Officer shall not pay to any who refuses to be so badged.

This had to be done throughout the country.

1726	To Eliz Renshaw to put in Spurrins (Banns)	0	1	0
	For going with Eliz Renshaw to take Illingworth	0	1	0
	For ye warrant	0	2	0
	Charges then	0	1	4
	To two men for attending him	0	2	0
	Charges that night	0	3	0
	To Illingworth in money	0	5	0
	For ye Wedding and charges	0	8	2
	For going with them to be married	0	1	0
	For mending Eliz. Renshaw shoos	0	1	0

1748-9	For going to Kirkstall to see Jno Kirkham wife	0	2	0
	For a shift for her	0	2	6
	For an apron 16d. for a Blankit 3.9	0	5	1
	To ye Doctor	0	1	9
	For coals at severall Times	0	15	10
	For Harden for her Bed	0	1	0
	For Ale when she was laid out	0	0	6
	For Crape 18d. for the Coffin 5s.	0	6	6
	For bread and cheese 14d. for Ale 3s.	0	4	2
	Paid church dues 2.6 to ye Wakers 6d.	0	3	0
	Spent of ye bearers	0	0	6
	Gave their overseer for his trouble	0	5	0
	Paid for 30 weeks for her at 12d. per week	1	10	0
	For 11 weeks more at 18d. p.w	0	16	6

Illingworth appears to have been a reluctant bridegroom. John Kirkham's wife had obviously left the village, but since she must have originally lived here she had to be looked after or paid for by the Thornhill Overseers.

It is fairly clear that in the first half of the century individual help to the poor was by no means negligible. Later in the century the calls on the Poor Rate became so many that such individual care became almost an impossibility. Whilst the overseers spent £16 16s. 0d. in 1702, in 1802 they spent £880 3s. 0d.

The Overseers of the Highways Accounts

1725 Paid to Jno. Walker and partner for 285 ydsn of Cawsey 4*d*. per yd   4 15 0
For Ale when ye Cawsey stones was led   6 11

1727 For 14 yds of stone for ye Wells Att   3*d*. per yd.
To ye Draughts and Labourers when they led Cawsey stones   0 6 6
For 2 days repairing Ludwell Lane   0 2 8

1731 Charges at ye Bridge in Clegg Lane
For building and upholding ye Bridge for seven years   3 16 9
For drink when they pulled down ye bridge   0 3 10
(etc. etc.) to a total of   4 19 3

1746 To ye labourers for cutting a Ditch on ye Lees Moor, being 9 days at 10*d*. per day   0 7 6
For 22 days hacking at ye Edge End 10*d*. p.d.   0 18 4

1753 For Ale when they hacked at ye bottom of Cowms   0 2 0

1772 Dec. For Shooling snow in Deadman Lane and bottom o' the Edge   0 10 8

1790 May. James Longbottom for the footing of Smithy Brook Bridge   0 5 0
The Quarry filling up in the Mountain   4 4 0
73 roods of road making on Lees Moor at 10*s*. 6*d*.   38 6 6
Ale for the workmen   0 2 0

In the early part of the century "cawseys" took most of the money. They were put at the side of the execrable roads to give a firm footing to man or horse.

The ruts in the roads needed much "hacking". Later in the century an effort was obviously made to improve surfaces and money spent on the highways rose from £7 9*s*. 5*d*. in 1725 to £286 8*s*. 4½*d*. in 1801.

A Century of change

The eighteenth century saw the beginnings of great changes all over the country, and nowhere more than in the West Riding of Yorkshire, but the changes only really became noticeable during the last quarter of the century. When it opened social conditions were fairly static. Life for the original villagers was probably not very different from what it had been in medieval times. No doubt a larger proportion of them worked in the woollen cloth trade, but this they did in their own homes, and they grew a few crops and kept an animal or some hens as well. Any travelling they did was by foot or on horseback. It was almost impossible for wheeled conveyances to use the roads, which were rutted and holed in the dry season and quagmires when it was wet.

Imagine, then, this part of the West Riding about 1700. On the hillsides, almost limitless stretches of fields and grazing land merely dotted by farmsteads and upland villages; clear streams and rivers flowing from the Pennine moors to the valleys; in the valleys, a number of modest market towns (Halifax and Leeds the most important) thriving off the domestic cloth trade.

Now think of it as it is today – of Leeds, Bradford, Halifax, Huddersfield, Sheffield, and all the smaller towns between them; of their industries, with attendant factories and liberal deposits of grime; of the millions of people who travel easily from one of the places to another.

How was this transformation of the landscape effected?

First, through industry. As the eighteenth century progressed, improvements and inventions in the cotton industry were gradually taken over by the woollen trade. Power machinery was introduced, first using water power, and later steam. Astute business men, who had been acting as middle men between the home worker and the buyer were already making use of the labour of many more people than their own families, began to gather the workers together in mills which would hold the new machinery. At first it was only convenient to use power for the finishing processes, but gradually every step in the manufacture of cloth was taken from the home into the mills. The weaving of coarse woollens was the last process to transfer – the comparative weakness of the thread being the limiting factor – and it was not until about 1850 that the home weaver really disappeared, but by the end of the eighteenth century the transfer of all other processes was under way. When water power was superseded by steam, mills were built in the valleys in places where the population was sufficiently large to supply labour for them. The transformation of the modest market towns was under way, too.

Power machinery meant that far more cloth could be manufactured with an equivalent labour force, and eventually it was to be to the advantage of workers as well as management, but in the upland villages and separate farmsteads the disruption of the old established way of life meant individual tragedy to many people. Hand in hand with possible hope for the future came a real fear for the present, which culminated in this district in the Luddite riots in the early nineteenth century.

For a few years around 1780 the occupation of Thornhill men are given when their names appeared in the church registers. From them we find that about 40 per cent worked on the land and 30 per cent in the domestic woollen trade. Five per cent are given as colliers. The rest are spread amongst a large variety of trades and occupations.

Notice the colliers, "Coale-pitts" are mentioned in some medieval documents and in the registers, occasionally, from their start in 1580. When the domestic cloth industry disappeared, coal was to be of great importance to Thornhill people. It meant they had another important occupation open to them – below their homes, if not in them. In this way they were more fortunate than many similar villages, particularly ones to the west.

Occupations are next quoted in the registers in 1813. Out of 200 entries scrutinised around that date, 30 per cent, were still in the textile trade – but 22 per cent, were now miners. The next largest entry (9 per cent) appears under "spinster" – a measure of the illegitimate births, not a textile process. Farmers are reduced to four per cent of the entries, but now we find an Iron-Master, a millwright and two engineers.

To see where these changes were leading the figures for 1880 were examined (again 200 entries). By that date 33 per cent of the men were miners and only nine per cent were textile workers. Fourteen per cent were said to be "labourers" and the rest belonged to one or other of a very diversified list of occupations.

There were other changes. A widening of horizons in the eighteenth century through trade and war made it necessary to improve communications. First water transport-canals was improved and then roads. In 1699 the Aire and Calder rivers were made navigable as far as Leeds and Wakefield, and as a result trade flourished in both places. After 1750 canals were cut to join all the navigable stretches of all the rivers, and trade poured into the West Riding. By the end of the century, via the Calder and Hebble and Rochdale canals, there was a direct route from Hull to Lancashire passing through Thornhill.

From 1740 onwards efforts were increasingly made to improve roads. Turnpike Trusts undertook the repair or building of main roads, but local roads appear to have been in a shocking condition until the last few years of the century. However, communications generally were eased and the people of Lancashire and Yorkshire in particular began to move about to an extent they had not done before. Besides being a stimulus to trade this was also a stimulus to population.

The population was growing in other ways. There was an improvement in medical knowledge and increasing control of some of the killing diseases of the past. Diet improved with improved methods of agriculture and ease of transport. Also – a world-wide phenomenon – increasing industrialisation always seems to have brought along with it an increase in population. There appears to be an adjustment, largely unconscious, to the increasing opportunities of labour.

Using the parish registers with care – as mentioned in an earlier section – it seems as if there was in Thornhill, as in much of the rest of the country, a noticeable increase in births around 1740, and an equally noticeable increase in marriages around 1780. The marriages in 1780 are more than would be caused by the extra births in 1740. The combined result of these two changes, being cumulative, was that by 1800 the population was probably two and a half to three times what it had been in 1700.

To try to show what this increase meant to the villagers themselves here are a few entries from the vestry accounts giving the expenditure in specific years. They almost tell their own story.

Vestry Accounts for Township   For Parish

Year	Overseer of poor	Overseer of Highways	Constable	Church-wardens
1702	16 16 0	0 8 0	8 19 6	15 15 6
1706	13 5 8	(not given)	12 5 8	15 0 9
1721	36 12 11	2 9 6	10 14 10	17 13 9
1739	25 17 4	5 1 4	11 18 7 1/2	16 15 0
1748	50 15 10	6 19 6	11 0 3	26 4 4
1749	24 18 3 1/2	11 14 3	11 18 9 1/2	29 16 0
1750	31 17 3 1/2	12 5 3	11 9 0 1/2	21 4 11
1760	58 11 3 1/2	19 7 9	39 19 5 1/2	46 10 0 (a)
1770	88 17 10	25 15 1 1/2	16 7 2 1/2	37 13 6
1786	185 7 4 1/2	110 10 0	15 16 3	11 11 8
1795	214 16 1 1/2	170 1 5 1/2	32 6 4 1/2	12 11 8 1/4
1800	315 12 5 1/4	234 10 0	54 4 4	11 8 7
1802	880 3 0 (b)	—	—	—

(a) Includes £21 for a stable
(b) Figure obtained from County Hall, Wakefield

It is interesting to see that the Poor Rate was rather high in 1721. It was a period of poor harvests and in a decade of high incidence of smallpox. 1748 was another bad year, but apart from these cases the Poor Rate shows no startling rise until the last fifteen years of the century. By the beginning of the nineteenth, even taking into account the increasing population and decreasing value of money, the distress must have been shocking. The large numbers of children being born, along with insecurity in the woollen trade, must have been the main factors in the deteriorating situation. In addition, the very highest amounts spent followed years of poor harvests.

Notice also the increased expenditure on roads towards the end of the century.

Householders paid rates in proportion to the yearly value of their houses and land; the payments must have been a heavy burden at the beginning of the nineteenth century.

Religion and education must also be mentioned.

From the churchwarden's accounts, church finances appear to have been quite healthy until distress in the village began to be widespread. Much money was spent on church fabric. In 1724 a new loft was built and in 1777 (though requiring help from the diocese) a new nave. For many years the accounts show generous contributions towards ale and dinners taken by clergy and church wardens whilst carrying out their duties, and this liberal spirit was probably an indication of comparative comfort in village life. In the 1790s, however, such expenditure almost ceased.

Methodism appears to have started in the district in Briestfield about 1745. For a number of years only a handful of people were involved, holding meetings in their houses or in a barn at Whitley, but numbers would obviously increase over the years, particularly with increasing hardships. However, in 1764, in the Archbishop's Visitation returns – as mentioned earlier – the Rector, the Revd John Mulso, reported no dissenters in Thornhill. He also added when commenting on their attendance at communion ... "a very regular and decent congregation and no offense committed in upwards of four years that I have resided in this living". An enviable reputation! – even if the Rector might, perhaps, have been a little sanguine[6].

The Rector from 1767 to 1793 was John Michell, MA, FRS, who had previously been Woodwardian Professor of Mathematics at Cambridge University. He was an outstanding scientist and whilst living at Thornhill Rectory, he calculated the weight of the earth. His invention, the Torsion Balance, measured the earth's density. The experiment is now known as the Cavendish experiment but the Hon. Henry Cavendish, an acquaintance of Michell's, obtained the instrument after Michell's death and merely refined his result. Michell also made a telescope whilst at Thornhill which Herschell, the astronomer, bought after his death and used in

(6) Churchwardens also sent in reports on the state of the parish. Those still extant for Thornhill appear to be straightforward enough but I am told by Mr John Addy, PhD, of a Wensleydale parish where they said of a seventeenth century vicar that his sermons "were but a bibble-babble" and that they "would prefer anytime to hear the cuckoo sing".

preference to his own. Other visitors to the Rectory were Smeaton the engineer, who built the Eddystone lighthouse, Joseph Priestly, the discovered of oxygen, and Sir George Savile (Michell's patron), the able and popular Yorkshire MP whose outlook was radical in many ways for his day.

The Grammar School, founded in 1642, has been mentioned. In common with what appears to have been a trend over all the country, it seems likely that its influence waned in the eighteenth century. The increase in the working population at the end of the century probably meant that a larger proportion of people saw little or no value in education apart from the acquiring of certain elementary skills. Certainly the grammar school got into financial difficulties in the early nineteenth century and, in 1812, Walker's Free School was founded to provide a more elementary education.

Not that the villagers seemed to avail themselves of it very much for upwards of fifty years. It is possible, in quite an interesting way, to get what must be a fairly accurate picture of the amount of literacy in any place where the parish registers have survived[7].

After 1754 a certificate had to be kept of people marrying. Both bride and groom signed the certificate – with a cross if they could not write their name. Now, although it is fairly clear that reading was taught more often than writing in those days, if a person could not sign his own name when he was married, he could hardly be considered very literate.

Counting the crosses in the Thornhill registers in a period around 1755 showed 33 per cent men and 68 per cent women not able to sign their names. The situation then gradually got worse, the greatest illiteracy being around 1815, when 53 per cent of the men and 71 per cent of the women signed with a cross. Not until 1855 was it as good again as a century previously. By 1875 the figures were 13 per cent and 37 per cent, and in 1895 two per cent and eight percent. Nationwide elementary education for all had started in 1870.

To return to the eighteenth century. There are strong indications that Oliver Goldsmith was an usher at Thornhill Grammar School for a short time, most probably in 1756. Mr Joseph Ward, a well known Thornhill character who was born in 1835, wrote a letter to the Yorkshire press in 1911 in which he quoted what his mother had told him of her grandfather being at the school when Goldsmith was usher. In all points where the story can be verified (other names and dates he mentions) he is accurate, but, as yet, documentary evidence of the actual period itself has not come to light. Remembering, however, that Goldsmith wrote feelingly of the misery of an usher's life, that according to a contemporary he had spent some time in the Wakefield area, that Squire Thornhill is one of the chief characters of the *Vicar of Wakefield*, and adding to this strong circumstantial support from Mr Ward's story, it is quite clear that the probability that Goldsmith was here is very high.

So there is our picture of Thornhill through a century of change. One of the most outstanding things about it is the difference in poor relief in the Century – £16 16s. 0d. in 1702, compared with £880 3s 0d in 1802. But another is that during the last quarter of the century men were meeting at Thornhill Rectory whose ideas and work were to be important to the beginnings of changes even more sweeping than the eighteenth century had seen. Mathematician, physicist, chemist, engineer, astronomer, and independent minded politician – together they foreshadowed today's world. In today's world much remains to be done, but in Britain most descendants of those who suffered in the Industrial Revolution have got a share in the wealth that scientific and technological advances have brought in their wake.

(7) I am indebted to W P Baker MA for this method, demonstrated in *Parish Churches and Literacy in East Yorkshire*.

The Nineteenth Century

With the advent of the nineteenth century the sources for any local history became almost boundless. It is quite impossible to comment on more than the smallest fraction of what can be found. Many different avenues of research await later students. This writer freely admits to having made an almost haphazard and certainly very personal choice of material.

When the century opened the working people were often desperately poor, there was child labour, little or no education for the majority and no political representation without property qualifications. By the end of the century, whilst the state of the poorest was still pitiable, most of the nation had experienced a real rise in its standard of living. Houses were far more comfortable and convenient, child labour had virtually gone, education was compulsory for everyone to the age of thirteen, and most men had the vote. The Victorian age, in spite of many mistakes and some hypocrisy, was an age which cared for people's welfare, and it effected a revolution in social conditions at least as important as the revolution in industry of the previous era.

Luddite riots coloured the first years of the century in this district. The Napoleonic Wars added to the prevalent distress by causing the price of wheat to rise and export markets to be lost. It was very unfortunate that all this coincided with the introduction of machinery into the mills. Men who feared for their jobs broke the machinery they thought was taking away their livelihoods. Numbers of them went round the district doing damage where they could; in isolated cases they committed murder. Those who were caught were severely punished by death or transportation for life. After large scale trials of Luddites at York, John Batley of Thornhill Edge and Joseph Fisher of Briestfield were both hanged on 16 January 1813. John Lumb, an accomplice, was recommended for mercy and transported for life. It is not clear now, however, whether these men were in fact machine breakers or not. They were accused of burglary and of stealing arms at Whitley for which they dressed and behaved as Luddites often did.

After the peace of 1815 there was much agitation for the reform of parliament, sadly needed as a result of the growth of new towns and the new industrial classes. A man known as "Oliver the Spy" was used by parliament to foment unrest to the point of action in some districts, and then the ringleaders so discovered could be taken prisoner. Oliver spent much of his time in the West Riding and in 1817 he collected ten reformers at Thornhill Lees to discuss plans for a rising. All the reformers and Oliver were arrested, but General Byng, who was in charge of the local troops, knew all about Oliver and allowed him to escape. Fortunately, due to the astuteness of a Dewsbury bookseller named Willans and of a linen-draper named Dickinson, the whole shady business was uncovered in the *Leeds Mercury*. Oliver's Yorkshire victims were saved for Lord Fitzwilliam who tried the Thornhill ones, and Baron Wood, who tried the others at Huddersfield convinced that the plots were Oliver's, let the reformers go free.

An instance of the hard and sometimes almost animal-like life that must have been the lot of many people early in the century is shown in the following account. The incident, however, was obviously not without rough humour, took place on 13 September 1814[8].

William Heslam of Thornhill near Wakefield brought his wife to Wakefield Market Cross

---

(8) Account taken from *History and Topography of Wakefield and environs* by John Hewitt (1863).

with a halter round her neck and there publicly sold her to the best bidder. She was bought by John Blagg for 5s. Both Blagg and Heslam were well pleased with the transaction. Blagg and his new bought spouse then walked off in high glee, the woman enjoying the fun and frolic heartily and with greater pleasure than either the husband she had just left (with the intention of thus being separated from his for every) or the man who had just bought her as if she were a piece of merchandise – Blagg and this woman lived together after this public transaction as man and wife without any quarrels or regret.

It has been pointed out that the standard of literacy was very low indeed at that time – the lowest figure of all being in 1815.

The first schools to have any popular appeal were the Sunday Schools, which started at the end of the eighteenth century. As an important source of at least some secular education they lasted until attendance at day school became compulsory, though losing ground after about 1850.

The visitation returns of the first Bishop of Ripon, Bishop Longley (instituted 1837), besides giving details of church worship (e.g. "The colliers do not come to church" – at Thornhill) also give details of school attendance.

In 1841 the day schools were said to have 90 pupils and the Sunday Schools 280. In 1850 the figures were 106 and 250; in 1853, 160 and 200 and then – a turnabout at last – in 1856 they were 365 in day schools and 265 in the Sunday Schools.

But Thornhill had a mixed population and although working people of barely adequate means were no doubt in the majority, there were others whose standard of life must have been more comfortable. A Directory of 1822 includes as residents a solicitor, a steward to the lord of the manor, a woman who kept a ladies boarding school, a brass founder, a vintner, iron founders, two coal agents, a brewer, a boat builder, a horse dealer, as well as the more usual tradespeople such as baker, butcher and carpenter.

And a poster which has survived from 1823 shows how their children spent some of their time:

> Mr Hefford of the Free Grammar School respectfully announced to his friends that ... his pupils will recite the following selection of pieces in the schoolroom on Friday evening, the 7th November, 1823.

They included

> Alexander and the Robber)   by Master J.
> Pilgrim and Peas   )   Leadbeatter
> Three Black Crows   )
> True Monarch   )   (etc. etc.)
>
> The Night and the Glow-worm) by Miss
> The Orphans (etc.)   ) Marsden

After which Mr Collier's Ball followed when

> his pupils will perform a great variety of Ballroom and country dances ...

including

> Six fashionable Quadrilles,
> The Valentine Waltz, by Ten Ladies and Four Gentlemen, in which they will form the letters that compose the word Valentine,
> A Shawl dance by Six Young Ladies,
> A circular country Dance on a New and Elegant System,
> A garland dance by Twelve Young Ladies,
> Also several Waltzes, Scotch Reels, Hornpipes, Pas Seules, etc., etc.
>
> The room will be decorated and the floor chalked.
>
> Mr. C. trusts that the above dances are arranged in such a manner ... as to give

11. The Savile Arms in Church Lane in the early twentieth century. (KCS/SC/0771)

satisfaction; at the same time, he trusts that every allowance will be made for any Imperfections; the time of Tuition having been short; being only the conclusion of his first quarter. Mr. C's next Quarter will commence on the 14th November, when he ... pledges himself that no Exertions shall be wanting on his part to qualify his Pupils to excel in the fashionable and polite accomplishment of Dancing.

Tickets of admission may be had on Application to Mr. H. at the school.

Wise Mr C., to speak assuredly only about his own exertions.

Interestingly (in view of the account of Oliver the Spy) at the bottom of the poster are the words "James Willans, printer, Dewsbury."

A certain amount of parliamentary reform took place in 1832, but social conditions were still bad. For a time they continued to deteriorate rather than improve. Child labour in factories and mines was far worse than child labour in the home had been. Housing and sanitary conditions in the rapidly growing towns were so bad as to be almost indescribable.

But agitation for improvement was in the air: West Riding men, like Richard Oastler, the Revd George Bull (The "10-hour parson"). Edward Baines, editor of the *Leeds Mercury* and others, taking honourable part in it. Gradually the necessary reforms came, though some of them very slowly indeed.

Contemporary expression of Thornhill's reactions to some of the changes later in the century is to be found in the parish church magazines. It is fitting that the church magazines should be studied for, according to an historian of to-day[9], the mid-Victorian period was one of three times in English history when religion was indisputably a real force in the country's way of life. The serious nature of the problems being tackled and the sense of purpose in the work (as well as the enjoyment and fun of festive occasions which obviously never disappeared) clearly shows in the parish accounts – and in the general literature bound with the magazines. Some of the reading matter, stories or verse, seems over-sentimental or ever turgid to our taste, but there is no doubt of its effectiveness in telling a story or pointing a way to a better life.

From the parish accounts themselves, here is a quotation from the magazine of November, 1873, showing the educational position at that date.

It had recently been decided that to be half-timers children now had to be ten years old.

> The boys who work in the pit bank will be divided into two sets, one of which will be at work, and the other at school, week by week. The boys employed in the pit will be sent out every day at 12, so that they may have time to get to school at 2; to meet this arrangement, the Thornhill Boy's School (Mr. Dearden's School) will commence at 2, and half-timers will be admitted upon payment of 4d. for the fortnight."

The old Grammar School had finally become the boys' part of the Church Schools, and a new school built for girls and infants in 1869. The boys' school was enlarged in 1884. These schools were the result of the untiring efforts of the Rector, Canon Brooke (later Archdeacon) in the service of education. During this ministry he worked unceasingly to provide the whole parish, not only Thornhill but Shitlington, Thornhill Edge, and Lees Moor as well, with churches, parish buildings, and schools. (Flockton, Whitley and Thornhill Lees had been made into separate parishes previously). Thornhill church was given a major renovation and another new nave in 1877.

Over £40,000 was contributed in twenty years for these buildings. Canon Brooke and his relatives gave a very great deal of the money. He came from a family of textile manufacturers in Honley and all of them – his parents

---

(9) G L Clark in *The Making of Victorian England*.

and many brothers and sisters – were noted for their genuine kindness and unselfish lives. Clearly, they must have treated their wealth as a responsibility. Mr Henry Savile, who owned the family estates, gave generously too, as did the Inghams who owned the colliery.

The cost of the restoration of the Church was £12,000. When it was re-opened, in November 1879, £1,600 was still owing but the collections at the morning and afternoon services were £620 12*s.* 2*d.* and £81 19*s.* 5*d.* – which reduced the debt most healthily. One can't help suspecting that someone who wished to be anonymous put several hundred pounds into the morning's offertory but the congregation as a whole clearly gave to the limit.

Canon Brooke came to Thornhill in 1867. Writing in the magazine in 1874 about his first years in the village, he gives an entertaining account of his first service. Some of us may remember those Sunday School children later, after they became our grandparents.

> I shall not forget my first Sunday in Thornhill – the Sunday before Easter, 1867. It was on that day I read myself in and a large congregation had assembled in the church. But what a commotion – what a noise and confusion – what unchecked license of free conversation, as it seemed to me. Could this be the House of Prayer. And then, when I came from the Vestry, all the children of the Sunday School in the gallery seemed to jump up and stretch out their eager necks and a loud curious cry arose in the Church, 'Yonds him,' 'Yonds t'new Rector'.

But he adds that, very soon:

> I found that I had all around me warm kind hearts, on which I could depend for sympathy, encouragement and willing help in the work of the Parish.

Many of the important social improvements to the village took place during the twenty-two years Canon Brooke was here. In 1867, with the opening of Thornhill station on the old "Lancashire and Yorkshire" line, the railway came. In 1870 gas was brought to the village, and in 1871 water was laid on.

Here is another extract from the magazine:

> What a boon the water has been to us in Thornhill those know best who can remember the time when water had to be fetched from wells, sometimes as much as half a mile from the houses, and when in dry seasons, it was eked out at so much a bucketful.

In 1879 a petition was sent to the Post Office asking, amongst other things, for a second delivery of letters each day and the establishment in the village of a Telegraph Office (where messages would be transmitted by morse code). The magazine reports, "The petition has already borne some fruit. A second Delivery of letters from the Thornhill Post Office in the afternoon has already been granted, and it is hoped that some of the other improvements may follow".

Leaving the discussion of social conditions and returning to the middle of the century when the Revd Henry Torre was Rector, here is an account of a great storm which struck Thornhill on Sunday, 2 April 1848[10].

> Large angry-looking clouds began to darken the atmosphere, and continued to enlarge until about ten o'clock when distant peals of thunder were distinctly heard. As the hour of eleven approached, the flashes of lightning became more vivid, and seemed to emanate from two or three points of the heavens at one and the same time. Before twelve the rain began to descend in very large drops, and anon there poured down torrents of hail and rain, the lightning flashing and the thunders roaring in a manner tremendously awful, and thus it continued until near three p.m., when there was a slight abatement in the hail and

---

(10)   Taken from the *Thornhill Almanack* (1884).

rain, but only as it were to gather strength for a more violent and fearful elemental strife. About half-past three the storm began to rage and as if on fury bent, it exceeded its former violence and became indeed terrific. ... Hail and rain fell in such torrents that people living in houses situate below the level of the roads had much difficulty in preventing the water from flooding their dwellings. When there was an interval of a moment between the incessant peals of thunder, the sound of the descending hail and rain was truly awful, and the rush of water down the various watercourses resembled the noise of some mighty cataract. ... Such was the violence of the waters that some of the tombstones were literally driven from the places upon which they stood and some of the coffins, which contained the ashes of the silent dead, were exposed to view. The water, as it increased in quantity began to find its way into the Church in which the rev. gentleman was holding divine service at the time. Being pent up at the bottom by the fence wall, it flowed backwards into the chancel, through the chancel doorway. It also ran in a stream through the western doorway and down the aisle, meeting the other stream in the chancel so that in a short time a large quantity of water collected in the sacred edifice. The water now reached the top of the wall adjoining the road, and so great was the pressure that the wall was unable to bear the weight, and it gave way before the service closed and the pent-up waters rushed with terrific force across the road and fell with their full force against the wall and doors of the yard leading to the Rectory. These doors, although large in size and strongly made, were literally broken to pieces and the large stone gate-post driven down. Down rushed the water thickened with hail down to the Rectory. The person left in charge of the house, hearing an unusual noise opened the door to ascertain the cause and thus made way for the house being filled with water, she herself narrowly escaping injury. The house soon presented an appearance which is not easily described. A solid bed of hailstones was lodged in one room five feet in thickness, and the cellers were so filled that it took weeks of labour to restore them to their former state.

The Rectory was quite unfit for habitation and Mr and Mrs Torre had to stay with friends. It was months before house and grounds were restored to anything like their former state. It was Mr Torre who rebuilt the "Old Rectory" in 1824. Its gardens became a show place; people came in waggonettes from near and far to see them.

Mr Torre, who appears to have been quite a character, was Rector for forty-two years, dying in 1866 at the age of ninety. He was a relative of Florence Nightingale (who also lived to the same age).

In 1893 another disaster came to Thornhill, but a disaster of a more tragic kind. On 4 July that year there was an explosion at Combs Pit which killed 139 men and boys. Only seven survived out of the whole shift. Most families lost a relative. Expressions of sympathy poured in from the whole country and money collected for the dependents of those killed totalled £36,823.

Conclusion

This century has seen more changes worldwide than any previous one. Scientific advances have given us computers, nuclear power, men on the moon ... but in spite of all these things, and two world wars, much of Thornhill would still be recognisable to anyone who lived here in 1900. The changes that have most affected the lives of villagers are social and domestic – particularly the improvement of living standards. Homes with bathrooms, television sets, washing machines and every other electrical gadget imaginable, certainly would surprise a time traveller from 100 years ago.

In 1910 Thornhill became part of the newly extended County Borough of Dewsbury; but, although it is officially now one of the Dewsbury's suburbs, we of the village still retain a sense of independence in quite large measure. This feeling is helped by our geographically elevated situation, by the fields and farmsteads we still possess, and also, more inexpressibly, by the sense of our past.

The fields dwindle in number as new housing estates are built to house a growing population, by 1991 the population of the village itself was about 6,800 and of the electoral ward of 16,700. The passing centuries, and particularly the twentieth, have made us very different – in dress, occupations, leisure pursuits and, to a debatable extent, in speech – from our ancestors. But we still worship in the same place, walk the same paths and, in our gardens, till the same ground. In these things there is continuity.

Working patterns have changed since the Second World War. Textile mills and collieries which used to be by far the greatest source of work for local people, male and female, have gradually been reduced in numbers. At first there was diversification of jobs but recently, unfortunately, there has been unemployment in the area. The Combs Pit, the largest mine in Thornhill at the time, ceased working in 1972. However, there were mines at Overton and Netherton (in the old parish) still working in 1987 which gave work to some local men. In the strike of 1984-5 miners' wives in Thornhill organised support for the local mining community and, in particular, help for the children. So successful were they that the BBC reported on their efforts.

Throughout the century the parish council has been not only a main centre of worship but also of community efforts which have involved people from all sections of village life. The non-conformist churches – now, sadly, also reduced in number – have played their part, too. In 1952 the village produced a Pageant of Thornhill. It was the result of hard work and effort of almost every section of the community: churches, chapels, social club, colliery brass band, all were there; and it confounded the Jeremiahs by being a financial success. Thirteen thousand people came to see it. Amongst the many actors were a peer of the realm and a channel swimmer. Amongst the horses was "Roma", a white charger which had once been Mussolini's. After the final performance, to help to celebrate the week's success, Roma was taken right inside the Savile Arms. Even the weather behaved in a grand manner – cool summer evenings for rehearsals and the performances themselves, and, then, within hours of the end of the last one, a wind storm of such ferocity that little appeared to be left of scenery and scaffolding, next morning, except broken wood and twisted girders.

A village pageant is an unusual thing to include in a historical account which purports to be seriously intended, but the spirit of community it engendered, in these days when there is so much fragmentation of social life, was so

12. Thornhill Pageant, 1952. (Ex 52-2842)

strong as to be worthy of comment. For some happy and hardworking weeks, those of us taking part were aware of things we enjoy in common rather than things that divide us.

In 1972, to celebrate the twentieth anniversary of the pageant, the Thornhill Festival, lasting a week, was held. Amongst the numerous events one of the most impressive was the *Son et Lumière* performance in church, which pointed up its beauty and celebrated the story of the village.

Amongst other church events of general interest has been, in 1980, the erection of a monument to the Pit disaster of 1893 (mentioned earlier, when 139 men and boys were killed) and 9 September 1947 when eleven men were killed. In December 1980 a new ring of bells for the tower was dedicated. These had been transferred from a redundant church at Cross Stone, Todmorden, and most of the work of installing them was done by the ringers themselves.

13. The Nave (GJ)

A Guide to the Church of St. Michael And All Angels

by Barbara H. Nuttall

updated by
Revd Ronald W. F. Howell

Thornhill Church

There has been a religious establishment on this site since the Ninth Century, the time of Alfred the Great. Evidence of almost every period and style of building since then can be seen in the church.

Each part of the church is described, following a route starting at the porch entrance. Words or terms in *italic* are explained in the glossary. The bookstall area adjacent to the entrance is dedicated to the memory of Canon H.R.B. Coney, Rector 1940-1960.

14. St. Michael and All Angels Church, April 1995. (GJ)

The Nave

The nave and both *aisles* were rebuilt by G E Street between 1877-79. Street chose the Decorated style of architecture because it was the only period of which he could find no trace in the building. At that date the nave was Georgian, a rebuilding of an earlier one dating from 1777.

Note that the *font* is at a higher level and that the nave gradually slopes towards the chancel. This is unusual, but is dictated by rising land to the west. Evidence of earlier buildings discovered in excavations before the rebuilding in 1877, show remains of a much smaller building in the middle of the nave. It is likely that these date from a Norman or pre-Norman church built on the level ground. As the building expanded so it had to take account of the change in level of the surrounding site.

The west door is now concealed by a purpose built screen displaying fragments of stone from earlier buildings. More important than these is the display of Anglo-Saxon monuments which are the oldest remains in the building. Most of these stones were found during the nineteenth alterations, one of the largest and most important is built into the Tower wall. There are ten fragments – parts of Anglo-Saxon crosses and grave slabs. Four of them have inscriptions of which three are in runes, they date from about AD 850, and the inscriptions state from whom and to whom the monument was set up. They show that a Christian presence in Thornhill for at least 1100 years. A reproduction composite model of one of the grave slabs is on loan from the Tolson Museum in Huddersfield.

The windows in both north and south aisles are Victorian. Those in the north aisle portray the life of Christ as set

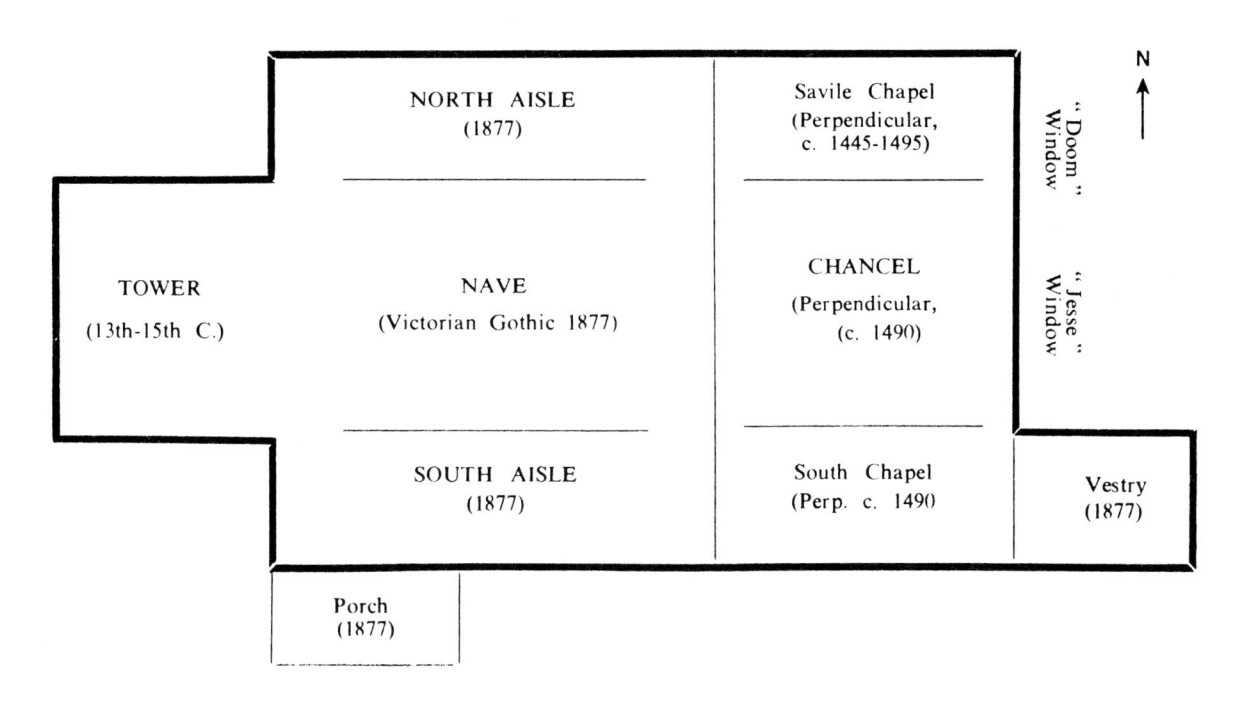

15. Plan of Thornhill Church.

out in the Litany; those in the south aisle are examples of some of the better work of the period. The north aisle is now partly filled by an organ, transferred from Crosland Moor Methodist Church, installed in 1981.

The *clerestory* windows are also Victorian and are inspired by the *Te Deum*. On the south side are the Apostles, St. Simon, St. Jude and St. Matthias; on the north side are the *Prophets*: Hosea, Joel, Amos, Obadiah, Jonah and Micha.

The *pulpit* carved from local stone, was the gift of the children and teachers of the Parish Church Sunday Schools in 1879.

The Chancel

Architecturally most of the obvious features of the *chancel* date from the *Perpendicular* period. They date from the time of Robert Frost, who was rector between 1482-1498. Frost was a local man who held many important church livings in plurality and who was Chancellor to Prince Arthur, Henry VII's eldest son. Prince Arthur died whilst his father was alive and his younger brother later became Henry VIII.

The Windows

The great east window is a *Jesse window* showing Christ's descent from Jesse, father of David. The stem of a vine rises from Jesse (two centre lights, bottom row) and spreads into all the sections where Jesse's descendants are depicted. David can be seen playing the harp and Solomon has a model of the Temple on his knee. The four major prophets, Isaiah, Jeremiah, Ezekiel and Daniel occupy the four corners of the window. The Virgin Mary with the infant Jesus and *Christ in Glory* are in dominating positions in the window.

The inscription reads:

> Pray for ye gude pperity, mercy and grace of Robert ffrost ccellor to ye redoubted Prince Arthur, 1st sonne of King Henry VIj, who was late parson of this church who hathe made new est window, and also clerestoried and archede this choir; finished ye yeare of grace 1499.

Note that besides putting in the window Robert Frost "clerestoried and arched this choir".

The east window originally was probably the work of French or Belgian artificers and is of very fine glass. It suffered damage through the centuries and was restored by Burlison and Grylls during the rebuilding of 1877-79. During the Second World War all the glass was taken out and stored in the local mine.

On the north side the clerestory windows continue the depiction of the *Te Deum* showing the nine *martyrs*; the south side has only one window filled but was intended to show the Holy Church throughout all the world.

Monuments

To the left of the altar is one side of a Savile *monument* – the rest of it being in the Savile Chapel. This was given in memory of Sir George, d.1614 and his wife Anne, by the famous Earl of Strafford (executed 1641). Lady Savile was Strafford's sister.

The figure in the chancel of a boy holding a skull and a book represents Sir George's elder son who died whilst a student at Oxford.

The only "brass" memorial is on a pillar on the north side of the Chancel. It shows the *escutcheon* of Philip Waterhouse (d.1614). He was a relative of the Radcliffes and lived at Overthorpe.

Note the memorial stones in the *Sanctury* – placed there during the restoration last century. Witton whose wife and son are commemorated) was parson during the *Commonwealth*. He was at sometime chaplain to Fairfax – the great Yorkshire leader of Parliamentary forces during the Civil War.

The fine wooden roof carvings were done in 1877-79.

The Savile Chapel

Nicholas Pevsner in his volume on *The Buildings of the West Riding of Yorkshire* says of the Chapel ... "it contains a remarkable number of monuments" and ... "much of the original glass remains. It has inscriptions of uncommon interest ...".

The chapel was built in 1447 and lengthened by one bay in 1493.

The Windows

The east window is a *Doom Window*, representing the resurrection of the dead and their admission into heaven – or hell. It is possible to distinguish figures being helped from their tombs: St. Michael weighing the souls; St. Peter with the Keys of Heaven and others. This medieval glass is said to be the best in northern England outside York.

The figures at the bottom of the window represent (1) William Savile, donor of the window, (2) his brother's wife, Alice Vernon (3) Sir John Savile, his father (4) Dame Alice Gascoigne, his mother and (5) his brother.

The inscription reads:

> Pray for the good prosperity, mercy and grace of syr iohn Sayvile and dame Alice his wife. The which William Sayvile enlarged this Quyre at his cost at the oversight of the said sir john hys nevew, wherewith pray we all that God be pleased. The which worke was finished in the year of Or Lord, 1493.

Sir John Savile mentioned was High Sheriff for Yorkshire in 1455 and 1461 and MP for Yorkshire in 1450 and 1457. He was chief steward of the Manor of Wakefield and, as such, in charge of Sandal Castle. He died there in 1482, "... was carried through Wakefield and sumptuously buried at Thornhill". (Hunter).

The two square-headed windows in the north wall formed part of the original chapel. Some restoration was done in the Nineteenth century; further work by the York Glaziers Trust in 1974. The window nearest the north aisle of the nave shows Christ upon the Cross, St. Mary and St. John. The coats of arms lower down are those of Dransfield (or Dronsfield), *quarterings* of Savile and Thornhill, and Leedes. In the Thornhill coat the *tinctures* are reversed.

In the second of the square windows are (1) figures of a father, mother and four children, possibly the family of Zebedee; one of the children is spinning a top: (2) The Holy Family – Christ, the Virgin Mary, her father, Joachim, and her mother, St. Anne: (3) Probably represents the Flight into Egypt.

At the bottom of the window the figures at prayer represent Sir Thomas and Lady Savile. The coats of arms of Thornhill and Savile can be seen in the folds of the lady's dress whilst Sir Thomas shows the quarterings on his breast-plate.

Translated from Latin the inscription reads:

> Pray for the soul of Thomas Savile, Knight, who caused this chapel to be built, A.D.1447.

The third window on the north side formed part of the chapel extension of 1493. It is a "Virgin Window" and probably was intended to show the relationship between the earthly life of Christ and the heavenly life of his Mother. The subjects in the three lights appear to be: (1) the birth of the Virgin and the Annunciation: (2) the Assumption of the Virgin and the Nativity of Christ: (3) the Coronation of the Virgin and the Resurrection of Christ.

Portraits of three bishops are seen at the bottom of the window.

There is a special two-part account of this window, written by James Fowler, FSA, in the first volume of the *Journal of the Yorkshire Archeological Society* (1870). It includes reproductions in colour taken from tracings of the glass.

Fowler discusses in detail the two lights, he was able to see at that time: the first was then covered by the monument to Sir George Savile, 1622. He also speculates on the first light and gives an insight, fascinating to read, into the reasons for the composition of such a window in medieval times.

Technically, he says, the window is characteristic of the fully developed period of Perpendicular glass painting – figures correctly drawn, altitudes easy, draperies simple but effective. Colour is used much more subtly than in the previous century.

Note, in the picture of the Resurrection, the four soldiers guarding the tomb. One is fast asleep, two are just awakening and one is awake but motionless with awe.

From what Fowler writes (before the Victorian restorations) it would seem that this window is the one which has survived best in its original form.

In the carved oak screen between Chapel and Chancel is the escutcheon in stained glass of George, first Marquis of Halifax. He was known as "The Trimmer" and was prominent in Parliament and at Court during the second half of the seventeenth century. The coat of arms shows the families into which his ancestors married: Golcar, Tankersley, Rochdale, Rishworth, Elland, Thornhill and Harrington.

Halifax was buried in Westminster Abbey and his tomb is in Henry VII's Chapel.

Monuments

The largest is the one already seen, in part, from the chancel. It commemorates Sir George Savile (d.1614) and his wife, Anne, sister of Sir Thomas Wentworth, later Earl of Strafford, by whom the monument was erected. The figure at the base of the monument corresponds with the one on the chancel side. This one represents Sir William Savile, second son of Sir George, to whom the estates passed in 1627 on the death of his brother.

Sir William fought bravely for the Royalists cause during the Civil War and was appointed Governor of York in 1643, but he died there in the following year. His wife continued to scheme for the King's cause, and an account of an attack by Fairfax's men on Thornhill Hall in 1648 is given in the accompanying history of the village.

The oldest monument in the chapel, the cross-legged knight on the floor, is almost certainly the effigy of Sir John de Thornhill (c.1260-1322) who obtained a market and a fair for the township in 1317.

The alabaster tomb-chest with eighteen weepers is that of Sir Thomas Savile (d.1449) and his wife. Sir Thomas was the son of Henry Savile and Elizabeth de Thornhill and it was he who built the Savile Chapel. He left money in his will for the erection of a tomb above him and his wife. The head of Sir Thomas lies upon a helmet bearing part of the Thornhill crest – a maiden's head crowned.

The oak tomb on the opposite side of the chapel is unusual in having three figures. These are Sir John Savile (d.1503) and his wives, (1) Alice Vernon, (2) Elizabeth Paston, a near relative of Henry VII. Originally the tomb would have a canopy and the whole thing painted in bright colours.

The inscription around reads:

> Bonys among stonys lye ful styl,
> quiste the sowle wanders war God wyl.
> *Bones among stones lie full still, whilst the soul wanders where God will.*

Sir John was Captain of the Isle of Wight under Richard III and High Sheriff of Yorkshire in 1486 under Henry VII.

Above that of Sir John de Thornhill is the monument to the first Sir George Savile (d.1622). It was executed by Maximilian Colt, sculptor to Royalty. Pevsner notes the excellence of the carving.

Sir George was married, first to Mary, daughter of the Sixth Earl of Shrewsbury (the great landowner and mag-

16. Monument to Sir John Savile and his two sons, 1529 (GJ)

nate who guarded Mary, Queen of Scots in Sheffield Castle) and she brought the Rufford Estate, Nottinghamshire, to the Savile Family as dowry.

The black marble sarcophagus which is the memorial to Sir George Savile, Seventh Bart. (*d.*1743) was the work of William Barlow, and is unusual for his work in that it bears his signature.

A slab on the north wall between the square-headed windows is to the memory of Sir George Savile, Eighth Bart. (*d.*1784). He was a famous politician of his day and known as "Independent Savile." He was popular and well-loved as a champion of the more unpopular causes. There is a full-sized monument to him in York Minster.

The most recent monument – a font, taking the form of a baby holding a basin – was brought from Rufford Abbey when the family gave up the house in 1948. It is a memorial to the second Lord Savile who died in 1931 and was made by Amy Lewis.

Most of the woodwork of the roof of the Chapel is original.

The South Chapel

Note in passing into this chapel from the nave a tiny gravestone of the twelfth or thirteenth century let into the floor. From the inscribed dagger it appears to have been that of a male child.

This chapel was added to the church in 1491 by the Rector, Robert Frost. Three windows contain fragments of fifteenth century glass discovered in various parts of the Church 1875-79. One complete shield of Amyas impaling Lacy can be seen. The memorial tablets on the walls are mainly those of the Elmsall family, locally important in the sixteenth, seventeenth and eighteenth centuries.

Part of the Chapel is now the Rector's Vestry.

In the arched recess on the south side (which probably contained an effigy at one time) is a tablet to the memory of Dr Lacy, Rector after the Restoration of Charles II.

Translated the inscription reads:

> William, Lacy, Doctor of Divinity, sprung from the most noble family of Lacy's, after that he had strenuously contended for the rights of the King and the Church at the great peril of his life and with the lamentable loss of all his property, and of liberty itself, was at length appointed Rector of this Church rebuilt from the ground the Rectory House which had been sacrilegiously thrown down, afterwards left the residue of all his goods to pious uses after paying his just debt, and quietly fell asleep in Christ, May 12, 1671.

Dr Lacy was at one time Chaplain to Prince Rupert, famous leader of Royalist forces. It is interesting to note that Lacy followed Joshua Witton to the living – and Witton had been Chaplain to Fairfax, equally famous leader of Parliamentary forces

Choir Vestry

The choir vestry is the nineteenth century addition in *Perpendicular* style. It has been divided horizontally to give storage at ground floor level, with stairs leading to the upper half which is used as choir vestry and meeting room. The alterations were made as a thanksgiving for the ministry of Revd Nicholas Webb, Rector from 1970 until his death in 1992.

South Aisle

The windows are good examples of nineteenth century stained glass and were given as memorials by local families. They illustrate the "Ministry of the Holy Angels". The eight subjects in the upper panels are taken from the *Old Testament*; those in the lower panels from the *New Testament*. Between these two sets are represented eight of the nine orders of angels. It was decided to take angels as the subject for these windows since it seemed to the builders and restorers of 1877, from such remnants as they found, that there might at one time have been an "Angel Chapel" in the Church – probably the South Chapel.

The Tower

Passing to the Tower from the South Aisle – the windows in the West Wall close by the porch are Baptism Windows. They show *John the Baptist* and St. Philip, the *deacon* from the New Testament, and *Noah* and *Moses* from the Old Testament.

The font is a memorial to the Revd Henry Torre, Rector 1825-1866. He was a cousin of Florence Nightingale. There are memorial tablets on the wall to the Radcliffe family and the Revd John Michell, Rector 1767-1793.

The Radcliffes lived at Overthorpe Hall. George Radcliffe (1593-1657) was attorney and friend to the Savile family and to the Earl of Strafford. He died in exile in Flanders during the Commonwealth.

The Revd John Michell had been a Professor of Mathematics at Cambridge before coming to Thornhill. Whilst he was here he continued his scientific work. This included the invention of the Torsion Balance by means of which he found the weight of the Earth, he also did important work in optics, magnetism and geology.

Architecturally, the base of the Tower is probably the oldest part of the present church (see external doorway) – but the battlemented top is of the Perpendicular period, and perhaps early fifteenth century.

In December 1980, a new ring of 8 bells was dedicated. these were transferred from Cross Stone, Todmorden. These replaced the six bells given by Captain Ingham of Overthorpe which themselves replaced three older ones, one of which was dated 1634.

List of Rectors

This can be seen on the wall near the Tower steps. Amended slightly, the list should now read:

c.1175	Germanus de Thornhill
c.1190	Jeremiah de Thornhill
c.1212	Germanus II
Early 13th Century	Ricardus
Later 13th Century	Gilbert de Bingley
1290	Will de Burge
1318	Henry de Spennithorne
1342	John de Thornhill
1402	William Thornhill
1418	Rad. Pillary vel Pesseleu
1433	Robert Hall
1482	Robert Frost
1498	Thomas Peck
1513	Thomas Alyne
1558	John Rudde
1578	Edw. Whitacars
1612	Charles Greenwood
1644	James Hannay, D.D.
1645	Joshua Witton
1662	William Lacy, D.D.
1671	John Savile
1701	John Anby
1714	John Copley
1732	Henry Elmsal
1759	John Sandford
1760	John Mulso
1767	John Michell, F.R.S.
1793	Hon. John Lumley
1813	Matthew Dixon
1824	Henry Torre
1867	Joshua Ingham Brooke (Canon and Archdeacon)
1889	Frederick R. Grenside (Canon)
1907	Henry T. Hayman (Canon)
1940	Harold R. H. Coney (Canon)
1961	Christopher G. H. Spafford
1970	Nicholas D. J. Webb
1993	Ronald W. F. Howell

Porch

Note the porch to the south door. Although a Victorian copy of the Decorated style, it includes beautiful carvings of foliage, fruit and flowers, and angels as they adore Christ in Glory.

Parish Chest

The Church no longer has its ancient Parish Chest but it still has the plate and documents that the chest would originally have held.

Plate

The oldest piece is a silver Charles II Chalice, 9 1/2" high, inscribed "THORNEHILL COMMUNION CUPP", Anno Dom 1663". This was clearly a *Restoration* piece. Very little Church plate of earlier times survived the *Commonwealth*. There is also a very fine silver paten, 8 inches in diameter, inscribed "This piece of plate was given to Thornhill Church by Sir John Armytage, Bart., of Kirklees". The hallmark is 1711-12 (Sir John was married to Margaret Thornhill of Fixby, a descendant of a junior branch of the original Thornhill family).

17. Thornhill Church Communion Plate. The chalice dates from 1663. (GJ)

Three pewter patens inscribed "THORNHILL COMMUNION PLATE" and a pewter alms dish were made about 1690. In 1896 Frederick Gill, the last of his line, gave, in memory of his forbears, a silver gilt Communion Set, including a chalice and paten and two silver and glass flagons, the hallmark being 1895-6. These were made from old family plate.

Other pieces, including altar ornaments and font ewer, have been given during this Century.

Documents

Only nine years are missing from the virtually complete set of Parish Registers which date from 1580.

There are two large volumes of Vestry Accounts dating from *c*.1680 into the nineteenth century. These give a remarkably interesting picture of life in the village over those 150 years. They include accounts by Churchwardens, Constable, Overseers of the Poor and Overseers of the Highways (See *History of Thornhill*).

These records are now deposited with the West Yorkshire Archive Service in Wakefield and may be seen by prior arrangement.

Outside

Gravestone inscriptions from the north east of the churchyard have been recorded, and in 1980 the area was grassed. At the same time a car-park was created at the east end, and the war memorial moved to a new site. A further monument was erected to commemorate the victims of the pit disasters of 1893 when 139 people were killed, and that of 1947 when 11 men lost their lives. The National Coal Board gave a seat.

A Geology trail to the churchyard is also available.

This building has a long history. It shows in wood, stone and glass what men and women have believed about God and about his purpose for them. It is a visible reminder of their faith and faithfulness.

Before you leave, please pause and remember:

to thank God for his blessings upon you, remembered and forgotten;

those who have built this place, and those whose prayers have made it holy; those whose lives have been the work and witness of the Church in this parish; those who seek to be the Body of Christ here, today.

Grant us to know and show God's love to find and to be Christ's presence in the world.

GLOSSARY

aisle: usually added to the nave to give more space aisles are parallel to the nave, but separated from it by pillars. The word comes from the Latin for *wing*.

angel: angels according to tradition are messengers between man and God. They are divided into nine orders of groups depending on their particular function. From the Greek word for *messenger*.

apostles: the original twelve disciples chosen by Jesus, including Matthias (chosen to replace Judas Iscariot) and Paul. Apostles were sent out as messengers to tell the story of Jesus to the world and comes from the Greek words meaning to *send* and *away*.

Christ in his Glory: Jesus Christ is often represented by artists as being raised on high in heaven as he speaks to his disciples on earth. (Based on Matthew 28: 18-20.)

chancel: the east end of the Church building containing the choir, clergy and altar. It is often separated from the nave by a screen – in Thornhill this division is a low stone wall. The Latin word for lattice is *cancellare*, hence this screen is the origin of *chancel*

clerestory: literally means *clear-storey*. It refers to the upper row of windows in the nave, above the roof of the aisles, where the windows are left clear letting in the light.

Commonwealth: the period following the Civil War when Oliver Cromwell and Parliament ruled in the place of a King. It lasted until the Restoration of Charles II in 1660.

Decorated style: a period of English architecture from 1307-1377 so called because windows and roofs in particular are more highly decorated than previously.

Doom: from the Old English word *Dom* meaning judgement. Doom refers to the Last Judgment, when good people will be sent to heaven and the wicked to hell. It was a popular subject in medieval art and usually painted on the arch above the chancel.

flight into Egypt: The story of Mary and Joseph taking the infant Jesus into Egypt to escape from Herod. They returned to Nazareth when Herod died. (Matthew 2: 13)

font: comes from the Latin word *fons* meaning fountain or source. It is a container, usually stone, for holding water being used in baptism.

G E Street: 1824-1881. A leading architect who specialisied in church buildings in the Gothic Revival style which was based on medieval designs but interpreted in a Victorian way.

Jesse Tree: the *family tree* of Jesus tracing his ancestry through the line of David. The tree is usually shown as a vine, and the stem does not usually touch Jesus, to indicate his divinity. Jesse in Hebrew means *God* or *God exists*.

John the Baptist: Living in the desert John the Baptist called for repentance, preparing the way for Jesus, whom he baptised in the River Jordan. He was beheaded by Herod.

Litany: the form of prayer consisting of a series of requests to God said or sung, with congregational response. In the Church of England it is appointed to be used on certain days of the week after morning prayer.

martyrs: the name given to those who suffered hardship and death for their witness as Christians. The word comes from the Greek meaning *witness*.

monument: from the Latin to *remind* or *warn* meaning *that which calls to mind*. It is a tablet or tombstone or construction to the memory of someone who has died. Many monuments show the mourning family of the deceased: others have reminders of mortality – skulls, cross bones, a scythe or hour-glass; occasionally they reflect the piety or generosity of the deceased.

Moses: the founder and law giver of Israel he led the Israelites from slavery in Egypt to freedom in the Promised Land. It was through Moses that God made his *covenant* or bond with his people, when he *chose* them to be his own.

nave: the area of the church building where people sit. Comes from the Latin *navis* meaning ship – an image of the Church saving people from the perils of life.

New Testament: the second, shorter section of the Bible which tells of the life, death and Resurrection of Jesus and the growth of the early Church. Originally written in Greek the New Testament tells of the new *covenant* or agreement made between God and man through Jesus.

Noah: tenth in the descent from Adam according to the story in the book of Genesis. Noah, warned by God that a flood would cover the earth, built the Ark and rescued specimens of all living creatures.

Old Testament: this is collection of writings which the Christian church shares with the Jews. They are the larger part of the Bible and tell of God's dealings with his people over many, many years before the birth of Christ.

Perpendicular: the period of English architecture popular between 1388-1485. Following the decorated style with the common feature of upright lines in the window bars and in the panelling.

Philip, the deacon: sometimes called Evangelist should not to be confused with Philip the apostle. Philip the deacon is mentioned in the Acts of the Apostles (Acts 8:5,26,35; 21:8).

prophets: men and women inspired to deliver messages directly from God, often about the future, but also to their own time, where they reminded people of their failure to recognise God's presence in the world and in their lives.

pulpit: derived from the Latin word meaning *stage, platform* or *scaffold*. The pulpit is raised so that the congregation in the nave can see and hear the preacher.

sanctuary: the part of the Chancel within the altar rails where the altar is found, the word comes from the Latin *Sanctus* meaning holy.

sarcophagus: was originally derived from a sort of limestone used by the Greeks in the making of coffins which was said to allow the flesh to disintegrate quickly. The word is now used of any large stone coffin containing inscriptions relative to the deceased. It is usually found above the actual grave.

Te Deum: a Latin hymn of praise to God and his son, Jesus.

tincture: in heraldry the colours, metals or furs used in a coat of arms

BIBLIOGRAPHY

Baker, W P, *Parish registers and illiteracy in East Yorkshire*, East Yorkshire History Society, (1961).

Clark, George, S R K, *Making of Victorian England*, Routledge, (1991)

Clay, C T, "The family of Thornhill: the main line" *Yorkshire Archeological and Topographical Journal*, vol. 29, (1929).

Fowler, James, "On the painted glass at Thornhill", *Yorkshire Archeological and Topographical Journal*, vol. 1, (1870).

Halifax, George Savile, Marquis of, *Complete Works*, Penguin Classics Series, (1969).

Hewitt, J, "*History and topography of the Parish of Wakefield* and environs (1863).

Leeds Mercury

Pevesner, Nikolaus (ed.), *Yorkshire West Riding* in the Buildings of England Series, Penguin new ed. (1970).

Thornhill Almanac (1884)

Whitaker, T D, *Loidis and Elmete*, Leeds, (1816).

INDEX

Agriculture, 7, 20, 33, 37
Anglo-Saxon, 2, 3, 49
Archbishop's Visitation, 35
Armytage, Sir John of Kirklees, 56
Ash Furshott, 15, 24
Assize Rolls, 9

Baines, Edward, 40
Batley, John (Luddite), 37
Bersuith, 2
Binns, Revd Antony, 13
Bishop's Visitation, 38
Black Death, 7
Briestfield, 26, 28, 35
Brooke, Revd Joshua Ingham, 40, 41
Bull, Revd George, 40
Byng, General, 37

Canals, 34
Canterbury Cathedral, 5
Cavendish, Hon. Henry, 35
Census 1801, 26
Church restoration 1878-9, 41, 50, 54
Churchwardens, 20, 23, 29, 30, 35, 57
Civil War, 14, 18-19, 52
Coal and colliers, 33, 34, 38, 40, 41, 43
Combs Pit disasters, 42, 43, 45, 57
Constable, 9, 20, 29, 30, 35, 57
Constable's Accounts, 35
Cookson, Anne, 13
Court rolls, 8, 20, 23

Danes, invasions, 2
De Laci, Ilbert, 4
De Thornhill, Elizabeth, *b.*1365, 10, 52
De Thornhill, Henry, late 13th century, 9
De Thornhill, Sir Brian, 6
De Thornhill, Sir John *c.*1260-1322, 5, 6, 8, 10, 52
De Tornil, Jordan, 5
Dewsbury, 1, 3, 4, 7, 8, 9, 25, 43
Domesday Survey, 3, 4
Drake, Tobias, 23

Edge Lane, 15
Edmonds, Thomas (of Wentworth Woodhouse), 13
Education, 23, 25, 35, 36, 37, 38, 40

Elmsall family, 17, 54
Elmsall, Henry, Rector 1732-1759, 17
Elmsal, William, lawyer, *d.*1740, 17
Essolf, 5

Fairfax, Colonel Charles, 18-19, 50, 52
Fisher, Joseph (Luddite), 37
Flockton, 3, 4, 5, 7, 9, 25, 26, 28, 40
Frost, Revd. Robert, 10, 13, 23, 50, 54

Gerneber, 4
Gilsuith, 2
Goldsmith, Oliver, 36
Grammar School, 25, 36, 38, 40
Greenwood, Revd Charles, 13, 23

Half-timers, 40
Hardcornfield, 20
Hearth Tax, 1666, 25

Industrial Revolution, 33, 36, 37

Kings Demesne, 3
Kirkenfield, 15, 24

Lacy, Revd Dr William, 25, 54
Lees Hall, 17
Lees Moor, 40
Luddites, 33, 37
Ludwell Field, 15, 24
Lumb, John, (Luddite), 37

Manorial Courts, 8
Market, 6
Methodism, 35
Michell, Revd John, 35, 55
Middle Coal Measure, 1
Miners' strike, 1984-5, 43
Mulso, Revd John, 35

Napoleonic Wars, 37
Netherton, 43
Nettleton family, 17, 28
Norman period, 4
Northcliffe Field, 15, 24

Oastler, Richard, 40
Oliver, "the Spy", 37, 40
Osbert, 2
Overseers of the Highways, 20, 29, 32, 35, 57
Overseers of the Poor, 20, 23, 29, 31, 35, 57
Overthorpe coin hoard, 2
Overthorpe Hall, 17, 25, 50, 55
Overton, 43

Pageant of Thornhill, 43
Parish Registers, 26-28, 33, 34, 36, 57
Paston, Elizabeth, 13, 52
Paulden, Thomas, 18-19
Poll tax, 1379, 7
Poor Rate, 31, 35
Post Office, 41
Priestley, Joseph, 36

Radcliffe family, 17, 25, 50, 55
Radcliffe, Sir George, 17, 55
Railways, 41
Rievaulx Abbey, 5
Roman Britain, 2
Rufford Abbey, 13, 19, 54

Savile family chapel, 10, 11, 51-54
Savile, Edward *d*.1604 "The Simple", 13
Savile, Henry (married Elizabeth de Thornhill), 10, 52
Savile, Henry of Lupset, 10
Savile, Henry, *d*.1556, 13
Savile, Lady Anne (daughter of Lord Coventry), 14-15, 27
Savile, Lady Anne, (nèe Wentworth) *d*.1630, 13, 14, 20, 50, 52
Savile, Lady Mary (daughter of Earl of Shrewsbury), 13, 52
Savile, Sir George of Lupset and Thornhill, *d*.1622, 13, 52
Savile, Sir George, 1st Maquis of Halifax, 14, 19, 52
Savile, Sir George, *d*.1614, 13, 14, 50, 52
Savile, Sir George, *d*.1743, 54
Savile, Sir George, *d*.1784, 36, 54
Savile, Sir Henry of Bradley (Warden at Oxford), 10
Savile, Sir John of Elland and Tankersley, 10
Savile, Sir John *d*.1482, 51

Savile, Sir John of Howley, 17th century, 10
Savile, Sir John, *d*.1503, 13, 52
Savile, Sir Thomas *d*.1449, 10, 51, 52
Savile, Sir William 1612-1644, 14-15, 52
Sheriff Tourn, 9, 20
Shitlington, 3, 4, 5, 7, 20, 25, 26, 28, 40
Strafford, Earl of, 13, 14, 17
Street, G E, 49, 58
Sunday Schools, 38, 41, 50

Talbot, Lady Mary (daughter of 6th Earl of Shrewsbury), 13, 52
The Tops, 1
Thornhill Boys School, 40
Thornhill Edge, 1, 40
Thornhill Feast, 6
Thornhill Festival, 45
Thornhill Lees, 40
Thornhill map 1634, 15, 16, 20
Thornhill pit disasters, 42, 43, 57
Thornhill Rectory, 15, 42
Thornhill Rock, 1
Thornhill station, 41
Thornhill storm, 1848, 41-42
Torre, Revd Dr Henry, 41-42, 55
Torsion Balance, 35, 55
Town, the, ii, 15
Turnpike Trusts, 34

Vernon, Alice, 52
Vestry Accounts, 29-32, 35, 57

Walker's Free School, 36
Warenne, Earl, 5
Water, 41
Wentworth, Anne, 13
Wentworth, Sir Thomas, Earl of Stafford, 13
Whitley, 4, 5, 7, 20, 25, 26, 28, 35, 37, 40
Wife selling, 37-38
Willans, James, 37, 40
Whitton, Revd Joshua, 23, 25, 50, 54
Woollen industry, 7, 20, 25, 27, 30, 33, 34, 35, 43